What the River Says

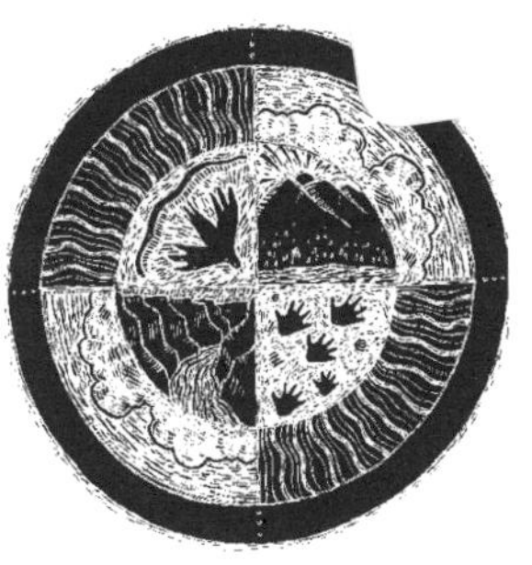

What the River Says

Whitewater Journeys Along the Inner Frontier

Jeff Wallach

Blue Heron Publishing, Inc.

What the River Says: Whitewater Journeys Along the Inner Frontier

Book design by Dennis Stovall

Printed and bound in the United States of America on pH-balanced paper.

Published by
Blue Heron Publishing, Inc.
24450 Northwest Hansen Road
Hillsboro, Oregon 97124
503.621.3911

10 9 8 7 6 5 4 3 2 1

Library of Congress Cataloging-in-Publication Data

Wallach, Jeff.
What the river says : whitewater journeys along the inner frontier / Jeff Wallach.
p. cm.
Includes bibliographical references (p.).
ISBN 0-936085-35-5
1. Salmon River (Idaho)—Description and travel. 2. Whitewater canoeing—Idaho—Salmon River. 3. Rafting (Sports)—Idaho—Salmon River. I. Title.
F752.S35W 1996
917.96'820433—dc20 96-21364
CIP

Ask Me

Some time when the river is ice ask me
mistakes I have made. Ask me whether
what I have done is my life. Others
have come in their slow way into
my thought, and some have tried to help
or to hurt; ask me what difference
their strongest love or hate has made.

I will listen to what you say.
You and I can turn and look
at the silent river and wait. We know
the current is there, hidden; and there
are comings and goings from miles away
that hold the stillness exactly before us.
What the river says, that is what I say.

— William Stafford

To everyone who's lifted a finger or a pen or a voice to protect the wild places that, while full of power, can't stand up for themselves in the face of ignorance, folly, and greed.

To Dory-heads everywhere—guides and passengers alike—who know the proper path.

And to Sue, with love, for seeing me through it.

Acknowledgments

A lone boatman working the oars of his dory. A solitary writer working a manuscript into shape. Neither of these actions is possible at the professional level without a world of support from others. My sincerest thanks to the following folks who helped make this adventure possible:

Curt Chang, Kay Metherell, and George Wendt, of O.A.R.S.-Dories, for offering me a full season's work, and for having faith in both my guiding and writing abilities.

The incredibly hard-working support staff—who often go unnoticed and unappreciated—at Boatland in Lewiston: Robin Chang, the family tag-team of Katie Whittman, Marci Whittman, and Shawna Whittman, and Marty Wellman in the office and commissary; drivers Arvid and Velma Armstrong, Mike Green, Ed and Mae Hanks, Bill Kempster, Marvin Peterson, and Dawn Whittman; shop worker Ken Hammack; and mechanic Tom Reece.

All the guides at O.A.R.S.-Dories for their support, instruction, ideas, hard work, humor, passion, and vision—especially those guides I was lucky enough to work with this summer: Remony Burlingame, Warren Case, Sky Davies, Rebecca Diehl, Barry Dow, Sandra Gaskill, Robert Henry, Eric Hudelson, Max Hueftle, Elliot Kuubits, Don Litton, Joel Mensik, Nikki Pace,

Andy Persio, Kelly Pettit, Chris Quinn, Trista Patterson, Brannon Riceci, Kurt Wald, and Leon Werdinger. Also Ric Bailey, Bill Bruchak, Pete Gross, Lonnie Hutson, and Nate Monschke, who contributed their thoughts and opinions.

On the literary side, thanks to my agent, Elizabeth Kaplan, and all the folks at Blue Heron Publishing, including Susan Skarzynski, Ingrid Opsahl, Bill Woodall, and especially Dennis and Linny Stovall, who have cared for and about this book since I pitched it to them, and who were brave enough to take a chance on it. And to the following readers for their invaluable comments, directions, and not always subtle opinions—they helped shape the manuscript, and their visions are expressed here, too (though the mistakes are my own): Ric Bailey, David Fishman, Brannon Riceci, Leon Werdinger, and, most especially, editor extraordinaire Sue Hill.

Contents

Preface: What the River Says

In the spring of my thirty-fourth year, sometimes I'd sit at night by the window of my apartment high above 96th Street in Manhattan and listen to the rush of traffic on wet pavement below. If I closed my eyes and let the sounds flow together into a single sound I could nearly conjure the rushing white noise of a river. This required a large stretch of imagination, as well as a few moments free from ambulance sirens and car alarms and people arguing on the sidewalk, but I found great comfort in the notion that moving water might be passing close by.

Rivers have much to tell us—through trickles and torrents and the gurgle of clear water flowing over smooth stones, through bird calls and wind in pines beside them, and the silent trails of shooting stars tracking above their circuitous routes toward the sea. Just as the river is constant yet always changing, it offers diverse commentary in different seasons, in various locations, in shifting weather, and to disparate listeners. It speaks in many voices, and what the river says is fluid. It encompasses opposites. It communicates in extremes ranging from placid to enraged, and its message may dip beneath the surface of consciousness, telling us things we don't yet even know that we've heard. What the river says is passionate, but it offers no conclusions. We must each figure out what the river says to us.

In my tiny apartment in that dark, noisy city, even the names of rivers—especially western rivers—were like ancient mantras to me, resonating clearly through the din:

Clackamas. Owyhee. Klickitat. Lochsa.

Salmon. Deschutes. Clearwater. Rogue.

There is just something about flowing water—rivers float an age-old nostalgia up to consciousness, changing us, reminding us of our undeniable connection to the earth, retelling stories we barely remember from our primordial past.

And if rivers can be metaphors—as they've been for writers and philosophers from Heraclitus to Hemingway—then a river trip, the journey of floating downstream, giving yourself up to the river's power, to the hypnotic rhythm of water moving over and against stone in an infinite variety of patterns: currents and eddies, waves and whirlpools, suck-holes and rooster tails...a river trip is another, more direct metaphor for the journeys that we make of our lives. The writer Paul Theroux put it this way: "There is hardly a boat trip in literature that is not also a metaphor for the active life... The greatest travel always contains within it the seeds of a spiritual quest, or else what's the point."

As taxis sped past in yellow streaks beneath my city window and red taillights curved out of sight beyond the concrete canyon's bend, I imagined myself borne away on the current.

And by early summer, when the snows were melting in the western mountains—in the Rockies and the Cascades and the Bitterroots—I made this real: giving in to the same instinct that inspired Huck Finn, and Conrad's Charlie Marlow in *Heart of Darkness*—the instinct to let the river take me where it might—I closed up the shop of my life and headed off to Idaho to work as a whitewater guide on the Salmon River, also known as The River of No Return.

I'd done some guiding before when I lived out West for a time so I was professionally qualified, and a company I'd guided for on occasion was willing to offer me a full season's work. But although I'd rowed and paddled more than a thousand miles as a paid boatman in the past, it had always been a part-time occupation, something I pursued on weekends, or for a week or two each summer. Now, I felt drawn to the Salmon, called from New York by its seductive voice to search for something in the clear, cold flow.

There are many reasons to pursue river guiding: the adrenaline rush of running whitewater, and the camaraderie among boatmen are certainly motivations. And guides are often lucky enough to share their adventures with great passengers. Like most boatmen, I also guide because of an inexplicable addiction to rivers, to that feeling of harmonizing with flowing water as I braid my own power with the stream to hit all the rapids right, to maneuver well—even artistically—through tricky runs, to experience a hard-won symmetry. But I also guide because I crave an elusive western dream, and the Salmon River is a rare place where I could chase it freely and believe that the mythical West still survives.

Throughout history, much of western exploration has taken the form of a search—whether for a route to India, or for the seven cities of Cibola, for wealth, land, gold, or sites for railroads or hydropower dams. But the great western myth suggests that early explorers were also searching for something more elusive: freedom, individuality, a chance to interact with a wild landscape, to live with it and within it. The myth assures us that just over the next ridge lies someplace better and lovelier, where the rivers speak lyrically and the nights are always gentle and warm. Where we can remake ourselves and start anew. Going to that romanticized place is far less important than believing that such a distant territory awaits our arrival somewhere on the blue horizon.

Restlessness and westward movement toward the wild lands and waters beyond the 100th meridian helped create and define the American character. But it may well have been the mythic West, the *idea* of the wild West, too, that attracted pioneers and mountain men, trappers and cowboys, miners and homesteaders, men and women who went West to grow up with the country, and in so doing, contributed even further in building up a myth of such staggering proportion and power that late in the twentieth century—in an era when the last, best places have been besieged by fast-food franchises and strip malls, when the forests have been logged, the rivers dammed, and the remotest outposts paved over and built up with souvenir shops—we may be lost without that myth. We need it far more now than we did a century or even a decade ago. A cultural Alzheimer's has settled upon the nation, and we don't know where to turn for our inspiration, to set our souls free, to experience wildness, to remind us of who we are and who we could be. Although today the myth—like much of the once-pristine western environment—needs some restoration work, it's still vital to us as a nation and as individuals.

My instinct to head West for an entire summer was born of similar desires for an elusive wildness, for a chance to live at the frontier for a while. I wished to become an explorer—if not of uncharted geographical terrain, then of the territory within. Like so many others called West, I was searching for something, too; the river seemed to whisper across a great distance, in the hush of New York traffic, that I might discover it in flowing water.

River guiding requires boatmen to read the water, discerning which waves and white curls contain hidden boulders or sharp spires of rock, where the current will carry you, where to resist it, where to pivot the boat, which is the safest route through a maze of obstacles. Each run constitutes a trip into unknown terrain because the river changes with every fluctuation in water level. The key to guiding a boat safely through rapids is understanding the physics of flow and applying your own energy in smooth confluence. You must become a part of the river, must think and react spontaneously, with the natural abandon of moving water.

Reading the river and picking out such signs, hearing what it has to say at a particular moment, in a particular place, is the secret to intimacy, to knowing the Salmon's hidden underside—the channel it has carved, where it flows over rock, where it flows over sand. Reading the river, we also learn how to know ourselves, and that is much of what drew me to guiding this summer. Deciding just how to run a rapid is an act of pure exploration and individualism, and much of what whitewater boating—or any activity pursued along a wild and uncertain frontier—is all about.

I spent most of my summer days rowing baggage and passengers, in rubber rafts and fragile, hand-crafted dory boats, in hot sun and cold rain on the clear green water of the Salmon—eight trips between June and August. I spent most of my nights sleeping on sandy beaches under black star-flecked skies. The sound of the river came to me like...well...like the sound of a river.

Several excellent books, maps, and guides have been published describing the physical aspects of such trips along the Salmon. These offer advice on running rapids and provide historical detail regarding who homesteaded the creeks, who shot who for his horses or his furs, who drowned, and where, while trying to cross the stream on a cable in winter. I refer readers to Robert Bailey's original 1947 book, *River of No Return*, and to another by the same name, extensively researched and written with down-home humor by Johnny Carrey and Cort Conley in 1978.

This book, however, sets out to describe different terrain. If previous volumes concerned themselves with the physical river journey, I mean to address the metaphysical journeys that participants on any river trip undertake. If previous books discuss the current, this one describes the undercurrents. I like to think of it as an inner guidebook to river trips. The book's structure parallels that of the river—sometimes leisurely and reflective, sometimes quick and exhilarating—as it winds through the wilderness, always cutting deeper into the topography. I've sought to move beneath the surface splendor and sudden thrills of river running to get at the powerful depths of the experience, namely how and why a week on a wilderness river manages to touch so many people so profoundly.

I don't mean to suggest that one full season of guiding has revealed even a fraction of the river's secrets. My perspective is as much that of a journalist as of a professional guide. Although my rowing skills were adequate (I didn't lose a single passenger), I didn't even know how to bake a peach cobbler in a Dutch oven, or tie a respectable bowline knot, both of which constitute requisite boatman's skills. I owe a debt of gratitude to the many guides I worked with; they answered my questions with great patience, taught me what I needed to learn, and didn't laugh too hard when I ruined an instant cheesecake for dessert or forgot to tie my boat when we pulled up on shore.

River guides never seem to give a thought to compromise; they endure difficulty for the chance to live the way they want, working outdoors in beautiful places, connecting to people in ways that just aren't likely any more. They work harder than anyone I've known, most of them, for little obvious reward: the money is negligible and the hours are long. I feel honored to have worked beside them, and will always remember their kindness and dedication.

On our journeys down The River of No Return, guides and passengers alike spend our days trying to get close to the river: we ride on it, swim in it, and cool off in its depths. We drink and cook with it and use it to purify ourselves. Loren Eiseley wrote in *The Immense Journey*, "If there is magic on the planet it is contained in water." The following pages seek to describe and distill some of that magic by considering what flows beneath the surface of a western river journey, and below the surface of the river itself, all the way down to the gravel where salmon spawn.

I hope to communicate—with even a fraction of its own grace—some of what the river says.

Portland, Oregon
March, 1996

Put-in: The River of No Return

"We can have wilderness without freedom; we can have wilderness without human life at all; but we cannot have freedom without wilderness."
EDWARD ABBEY

"Wilderness opens our minds, gives us freedom, and allows us to expand. The times spent, and those many yet to be spent, in the far backcountry ignite our imagination: the craggy vista that the topography tells us should open up not much farther ahead; a hushed, sundown time, inlaid with the sacred, looking down into a red-rock, sagebrush canyon; a true chance, along with the edge of danger, that if we play it right, a humped grizzly may soon be feeding and romping in the berry patch at the upwind end of the meadow. Our reactions to the wild land are dignified and deserving. They call to the same parts of us as the vibrant exhibition of the French Impressionists of a year past, the long prayer in a steepled church in that time of pain and confusion, and that classic book of a faraway place read on a slow-moving childhood summer day. Wilderness is manifested in physical places but it also has to do with the mind, with expression, with self.

"All of this is especially true in the American West. Wilderness is a peculiarly western institution."
CHARLES WILKINSON, *THE EAGLE BIRD*

Idaho's Salmon River gathers its waters from tributary streams flowing out of the rugged Sawtooth and Salmon River Mountains in the south, the Clearwater and Bitterroot Mountains to the north, and from Big Redfish Lake. From its headwaters to its confluence with the Snake River, the Salmon curves and flows for 425 miles, descending from an elevation of over 8000 feet to just 905, and averaging a drop of twelve feet per mile. The Salmon Canyon is the second deepest on the continent—second only to the Snake River in Hell's Canyon—and one-fifth deeper than the Grand Canyon. For a length of 180 miles, the Salmon Canyon stretches more than a mile from river to rim.

Following decades of dam building by the Bureau of Reclamation and other state and federal agencies nationwide, the Salmon remains the longest free-flowing river left in the continental United States. For eighty miles between Corn Creek and Long Tom Bar, the Salmon—characterized by meditative calm stretches interspersed with difficult, muscular rapids—flows through a mostly pristine and breathtaking wilderness that is a microcosm for the frontier history of the American West. Designated by the U.S. government as a "Wild and Scenic" river (which offers it modest protections), it remains one of the few relatively untamed places left to us—eighty miles along which thousands of Americans have experienced a taste of wildness: by running rafts and kayaks and dories through boiling whitewater; by swimming in the cool river at midnight and howling at the moon; by dancing around a campfire while the deer watch, startled, from the yellow pine woods; by risking opening themselves up to each other and to the feelings that the river and canyon inspire.

In a 1904 newspaper article, local historian and writer Robert G. Bailey described the untamed and inaccessible Salmon as "a river of no return" because upstream travel was deemed impossible. The earliest river travelers heading downstream in search of homesteads, or adventure, or gold often dismantled their wooden boats and used the lumber to build cabins rather than transporting the crafts back toward their departure points across extremely difficult and mountainous terrain.

But some evidence suggests that the second trip ever undertaken on the Salmon, in 1867, was an upstream passage. In a world-class example of hedging, Bailey wrote: "It is called the River of No Return because it is impossible to go upstream the length of the river by boat. Laboriously, by pulling, poling, rowing, and portaging a boat can be propelled up the river, and it has been done, but it is such a task that for practical purposes it can be classed as impossible." Perhaps Bailey knew of other rivers on which upstream travel was an easy task, but even from the very beginning the notion of a "river of no return" might have been an exaggeration in the tradition of the western myth.

To those who've spent time in backcountry, the Salmon—in spite of its current designation as wilderness—exhibits far too many marks of civilization. On an average summer day, as many as four commercial river trips and several more private trips of up to thirty people each may launch on the Main Salmon from the boat ramp at Corn Creek. Even after pushing off into the current and disappearing around the corner into the Wild and Scenic corridor, passengers will glimpse occasional guest ranches, two primitive roads, a rustic telephone line, and plenty of other manmade "improvements." You might disinter signs of previous travelers on a beach, or beside your tent: cigarette butts, bottle caps, an apple core. And although the normally restrictive Wilderness Act of 1964 should have limited certain activities within this part of the Frank Church-River of No Return and Gospel Hump Wilderness Areas, a more recent act (The Central Idaho Wilderness Act of 1980) determined that the Wild and Scenic Rivers Act would take precedence. All of which is a long way of explaining how motorized jet boating was allowed because it was considered "historic."

Today (and since as early as 1947), jet boats can scream upstream the entire length of a seven-day wilderness float trip on the Main Salmon River in a single afternoon. Even if the Salmon had ever been a river of no return, jet boats and other signs of humanity now make the concept seem ludicrous and melodramatic—at least in the literal sense—except for one thing: not a single passenger who spends a week drifting beautiful flatwater canyons and darting through powerful whitewater returns home unchanged. Which suggests that "River of No Return" is appropriate when applied to journeys of a more personal nature.

I have watched our commercial passengers relax and uncoil out on the river to an extent I don't think they allow to happen much in the context of their familiar lives. In the serene, accepting, and sometimes disorienting atmosphere of the backcountry—where bear and moose and bighorn sheep may happen past camp; where time is measured by sunset and moonrise; where silence grows musical with running water—people discover the rare opportunity to confront their true selves. Participants always leave a river trip changed in some way. One reason they are changed, I think, is that the river presents them with a frontier experience—something rare in America in the late twentieth century.

Whether or not experienced backcountry travelers would consider the Salmon a wilderness, the river exhibits a pristine and unbridled nature. When you leave the trucks and vans and trailers behind at the put-in at Corn Creek there's no question about the remote feeling of the place. Spirited creeks pour their frothing waters into the river over boulders, slide down waterfalls, and draw your attention up whispering side canyons. Endless forested peaks and grassy slopes invite exploration. Ancient Indian pictographs provide mysterious comment. All while the river twists and bends through the canyon on its long voyage to the Pacific.

In early summer of my season guiding, the Salmon was at its highest stage in nearly twenty years, and that made it seem even more primitive and remote. It roared angrily through the canyon without restraint, brown with silt washed down side creeks, cold and violent. Many of the most ornery rapids were drowned under six feet of fast-moving water. By August, though, when the snow had melted in the high country, the river dropped from an earlier level of over seven feet to just half a foot. The current slowed, drawing familiar rocks up through the surface, and revealing the rounded stones of the streambed below. The river calmed, and grew pensive in places, though the rapids also grew feisty and more technical.

River rapids are rated according to their potential for upset and injury on a scale of Class I to Class VI. A Class I is nearly as flat as the water in a swimming pool; a Class VI is more like daiquiris in a blender, and considered unrunnable, "posing a serious threat of injury or death," according to the European rapid rating system, which is also used to classify rivers in the U.S. The Salmon's rapids—ranging as high as Class IV (except for the ominous Slide Rapid which was rated as high as V+ during spring's big water)—have distinct personalities: some are instigators, others are playful and kind as dolphins, still others are downright mean. And their names are evocative: Roller Coaster, Devil's Teeth, Whiplash, Dried Meat.

Once, there was just the river rolling through the canyon, and the rapids had no names. Eventually men arrived and named the side creeks and ridges and turbulent waters. Archaeological evidence suggests that the earliest inhabitants of the river corridor took up residence approximately 8000 years ago. They left behind pit houses, arrow points and tools, and occasional pictographs. The Northern Shoshoni called the river Tom-Agit-Pah: Big Fish Water; the Nez Perce named it Natosh Koos: Chinook-Salmon Water. But foot trails down to and along the river suggest that the Indians didn't navigate the waters much, considering it far too dangerous.

In 1805, those earliest of restless western travelers, Lewis and Clark, were likely the first non-Native Americans to come upon the Salmon River and consider running it in boats—until the local Indians convinced them to be the first of many whites to decide against it. Clark did proceed on land downstream about fourteen miles below the current site of North Fork before discerning it was unnavigable and opting for a difficult overland route of travel instead. Though he called it the Lewis River, after his partner, the name never took. On August 23, 1805, Clark wrote in his journal, "The River...is almost one continued rapid...passage with canoes is entirely impossible, as the water is Confined between huge Rocks & the Current beeting from one against another for Some distance below...At one of those rapids the mountains close so Clost as to prevent a possibility of a portage with (out) great labour...this river is about 100 yards wide and can be forded but in a few places. below my guide and maney other Indians tell me that the Mountains Close and is a perpendicular Clift on each Side, and Continues for a great distance and that the water runs with great violence from one rock to the other on each Side foaming & roreing thro rocks in every direction, So as to render the passage of any thing impossible. those rapids which I had Seen he said was Small & trifleing in comparison to the rocks & rapids below, at no great distance & The Hills or mountains were not like those I had Seen but like the Side of a tree Streight up...my guide Shewed me the river for about 20 miles lower & pointed out the dificulties."

Twenty-seven years after Lewis and Clark's sensible decision to head overland, trappers from John Work's Snake River Expedition probably undertook the first recorded journey on the Salmon. From the journal of that expedition, dated July 19, 1832: "The report we have among the Snakes [Indians] regarding our men who descended the Salmon River being drowned, unfortunately turns out to be true."

Not until forty years later, in 1872, did a survey crew from the Northern Pacific Railroad have a better time of it. The railroaders floated safely through in wooden scows upwards of thirty-two feet in length, eight feet wide, and steered by twenty-eight-foot poles fitted with oar blades. Fortunately, they found little advantage in trying to blast a track through the canyon; it just didn't make economic sense.

1872 was also approximately when the legendary Johnny McKay—the first frequent floater of the Salmon—made his initial descent. McKay journeyed to Idaho to help build a mill, but while showing off his work to his new bride, her skirt caught in the machinery and dragged her to her death. Seeking to face his grief in solitude, McKay adopted the lonely life of a placer miner along the river, which he traveled slowly some twenty times over the next forty-eight years, stopping here and there to work a claim for a while, or to hole up for the winter.

During roughly that same period, hardrock miners poured into the Salmon canyon seeking gold and providing a living for the first commercial river guides, who shuttled the miners and their equipment down stream. Harry Guleke, a well-known guide, charged $1000 per journey at the turn of the century—not much less than many outfitters charge today, and Guleke didn't provide wet bars and solar showers, as many modern river companies do.

In 1911, Caroline Lockhart, a novelist, rode with Guleke. Her descriptions of her boatmen perfectly reflect the mythology of the American West and the strong, individualistic heroes who most folks wanted to imagine inhabited that wild terrain. Recounting the return of two boatmen from a difficult trip, Lockhart wrote, "The return of two North Pole heroes never caused more excitement...And the Men themselves—the heroes of the people—Guleke and Sandilands—whose fame is nearly as wide as that of the river itself? Well they had the characteristics one likes to find in Men who do brave things—namely gentleness and modesty...Many are the tales they tell of [Guleke's] strength—how in an emergency, he broke a sweep in two, a tough green fir tree, to save a girl's life..."

Describing Guleke later, as he guided his scow downstream, she continued, "The wind blew his hair straight back and the joy of battle was gleaming in his eyes as he laid down on the sweep. His face was alight with exultation; he looked a monument of courage, the personification of human daring... The boatmen who have successfully pitted their skill and strength against the sinister power of the Salmon River can be counted on fewer than the fingers of one hand. There are now but two in Salmon City who can be considered pilots, and so great is the fear of the rapids that those who have made the trip either as boatmen or passengers are a comparative handful."

It was in a far more settled America, long after the "official" closing of the frontier and the initial rushes and ebbs of miners, that four men undertook the first inflatable boat trip, run solely for the wild adventure of floating the river, in 1929. As Carrey and Conley describe this trip, "The group was prepared for at least one eventuality because Joseph was a minister and Virgil was an undertaker." Six years later the National Geographic Society ran the Salmon, and in 1936, oar-boats began plying the waters, replacing the bulky sweeps. By the forties, outfitters offered commercial trips to adventurous folks who craved the sort of mythological western experience that was already becoming difficult to find in America.

In the nearly seven decades since four men first came up with the idea of running the Salmon for the fun of it, thousands of Americans have followed suit—outfitted with beach chairs and beer coolers and gourmet food. Their modern guides are no less a part of the western myth than were those first boatmen, or the scouts who led Americans west into the frontier a century ago.

As Wallace Stegner wrote in an essay called "Striking The Rock," "A generation ago, only five thousand people in all the United States had ever rafted a river; by 1985, thirty-five million had. Every western river from the Rogue and the Owyhee to the Yampa, Green, San Juan, and Colorado is booked solid through the running season. As the country at large grows more stressful as a dwelling place, the quiet, remoteness, and solitude of a week on a wild river became more and more precious to more and more people. It is a good question whether we may not need that silence, space, and solitude for the healing of our raw spirits."

O.A.R.S.-Dories—the O.A.R.S. part stands for Outdoor Adventure River Specialists, and the Dories part survives from Northwest Dories, which O.A.R.S. bought out a few years ago—the company I guided for this summer, runs river trips throughout the United States and the world, providing many opportunities for people to have transforming experiences inspired by silence, space, and solitude. I worked seven-day trips on the Main Salmon, between Corn Creek and the takeout at Vinegar Creek or Carey Creek, and four- or five-day trips on the Lower Salmon, beginning farther downstream and taking out at Heller Bar several miles beyond where the Salmon merges into the Snake.

The history books are full of great stories—true ones and tall ones, facts and myths—of the adventures and mishaps of the earliest river pioneers. But the stories of modern river sojourners on the River of No Return are equally compelling, funny, and full of implication: pioneers of a different sort and a very different time, whose experiences occur along another kind of wild frontier.

The Significance of the Inner Frontier

"...American history has been in a large degree the history of the colonization of the Great West. The existence of an area of free land, its continuous recession, and the advance of American settlement westward explain American development... The advance of the frontier has meant a steady movement away from the influence of Europe, a growth of independence along American lines...

"...And now, four centuries from the discovery of America, at the end of a hundred years of life under the Constitution, the frontier has gone, and with its going has closed the first period of American development."

FREDERICK JACKSON TURNER, *THE SIGNIFICANCE OF THE FRONTIER IN AMERICAN HISTORY,* 1893

"[The contemporary frontier] is immense and widely dispersed, however, so the journey there will take some time. You'll have to travel by land: commercial airlines fly to where people are, not to where they aren't. But the contemporary frontier can be reached. Far from the interstates and the cities they connect, far from the land of franchises and strip development and tract houses, even beyond the small but regularly spaced farm communities and their row crops is where a land-hungry nation nibbled but lost its normal appetite. Out there is the frontier, miles from nowhere."

DAYTON DUNCAN, *MILES FROM NOWHERE,* 1993

"The Salmon River is their own personal frontier, though obviously not the *frontier, because we can get them out. If you believe*

you're going to die, then you're scared, even if you're not anywhere close to dying. They really believe they're out there, on the edge. They see only one other group of thirty and they think, 'Oh, my god, there's no one out here.' I'm not going to spoil it for them and say we launched with 120 people and there's 120 more ahead of us and behind us."
BRANNON RICECI, RIVER GUIDE

It's a bright, warm, sunny morning at the Corn Creek campground and boat ramp, the put-in for trips on the Main Salmon River. Last night the temperature dropped into the downright chilly range, but already this morning the air is heating up, perfumed with pine and wood smoke and the scent of cowboy coffee brewing on a propane stove on the beach beside where we've parked our rafts and dories.

Four other guides and I are packing a few last items into our boats when we hear the crunch of a school bus lurching down the gravel road above. This is one of my favorite moments on any river trip: when the passengers arrive on that first morning. As I watch them climbing stiffly out of the bus, I know that although O.A.R.S.-Dories attracts many guests who've taken other river trips in the Grand Canyon, or on the Middle Fork of the Salmon, or on local day-trip rivers near their homes, this new group is also likely to include at least a couple of folks who've never floated a river before, and probably one or two who've never even camped out a single night in their lives.

Although I've spent a lot of time in the backcountry over the past ten years, as a former suburban kid and longtime city denizen I'm always drawn to these guests because I identify with their experience. When I was twelve years old I used to spend my nights reading river guide books, and looking at photos of western landscapes that were so epic as to seem impossible exaggerations. I longed for those places precisely because they were so unlike anywhere I'd ever been. Seeing our guests arrive, I know that many of them will find the terrain here equally as surprising. These are my very favorite passengers. I find their responses fresh and poignant, without a trace of self-consciousness. They are affected by the territory, and I want to reach out to them one by one and show each some small kindness.

Many of our passengers have just come from large eastern cities, and in the past twenty-four hours they've probably traveled on several successively smaller flights on successively smaller aircraft—let's say from Philadelphia to Minneapolis to Boise, for example, where they transferred to a plane about the size of a comfortable sofa with wings, which landed them in Salmon, Idaho. The town of Salmon is surrounded by a rugged mountain wilderness that would not inspire most travelers to hum catchy airline theme songs on a day when the weather is rough.

In Salmon, a van shuttles our guests to their motel. Not long after they've had a chance to fluff their pillows and try out the bed springs and peer into the bathroom, they're scheduled to attend a pre-trip orientation meeting. There, they'll catch a first glimpse of their fellow passengers and meet their trip leader (T.L.), who may very well appear wild-eyed from ten hours of driving from our base in Lewiston, Idaho, and attending to a wide variety of logistical nightmares. The T.L. will be wearing dusty river shorts and worn Teva sandals and a tee shirt that proclaims something like, "Attitude is Everything," or "Paddle or Die!," and chances are he'll appear at last slightly crazy and menacing.

The T.L. will introduce himself and then impart a thousand pieces of information that will prove crucial to passengers' comfort, but which they can't possibly remember. Then he'll distribute waterproof "dry bags" and waterproof military surplus ammo cans (which resemble children's lunch boxes) to hold folks' personal gear, and plastic thermal cups with the O.A.R.S. or Dories logos. He'll keep the meeting brief because of the numerous emergencies he must attend to. Following this orientation, and dinner in Salmon, most passengers probably climb into bed that night with pounding pulse rates, rushing adrenaline, and vague but grave doubts about the adventure before them—which is as it should be. Even experienced river runners must wonder what challenges this particular wilderness trip will present.

Six hours later, in the chill and the obscure light of an early mountain morning, they'll wake and eat breakfast and board the bus and drive from Salmon to the far smaller town of North Fork—last chance to buy Ibuprofen or chocolate bars, or to phone their brokers or life insurance agents. Then they'll head out on the road that parallels the river and degenerates from pavement to gravel and dirt as it approaches the put-in. Fourteen miles later they will bounce past the place where Captain William Clark turned back in 1805, determining that the river was far too dangerous to travel on. Twenty-three miles after that, the road dead-ends at Corn Creek, where they'll discover us waiting for them.

As they unfold themselves from the school bus and proceed uncertainly toward the boats, at least a couple of folks will still have absolutely no clue as to what they've gotten themselves into. One passenger this year asked me whether the bus would be waiting for us in this same spot when the trip was over, not understanding that next week we'd take out nearly one hundred miles downstream because rivers don't generally flow in circles. Another guest wondered if he could leave his family's personal gear in the bus during the day and retrieve it when the vehicle drove into camp that night.

It is this very moment when they step out of the school bus

and begin to lug their dry bags down toward the boats that perfectly epitomizes the notion of the frontier that has always been so important to Americans. As they shuffle down the path wearing goofy hats and spanking-new river sandals and aqua-socks, they're leaving behind every connection to everything that's familiar to them: planes and cars, telephones and fax machines, chocolate chip cookie dough ice cream and Tom Brokaw, video stores, poison control centers, and Quik-Marts full of extra batteries, film, suntan lotion, or other items of perceived comfort and solace. Ahead of them, down the sandy path beneath the pines at Corn Creek, a few boats are pulled up on the banks of a waterway often referred to as "The River of No Return."

These boats, and we guides strapping down coolers and dry bags, inflating the tubes of our yellow gear raft, sponging the decks of our dories, and arranging orange life jackets in rows on a blue tarp, represent their vehicle into the unknown. Ahead lie risk and adventure, dangerous foamy rapids and long difficult hikes, rattlesnakes and couscous: to put it simply, a way of living in which every single action that might have been familiar is new, and they'll have to learn how to eat and sleep and get a drink of water and wash a dish and even pee all over again, in a different way. This moment resonates with potential, as many folks straddle the cusp between civilization and wilderness, bus and boat, familiar life and dark unknown. Which is what a river trip is all about. I am moved by this every time, full of hope and anticipation that each of these people partly entrusted to my care might experience something they'll carry with them for the rest of their days.

When we proceed around the group in a circle offering a few words of introduction about ourselves, many guests admit this is all entirely new to them. I like to say that I've never been on a river before, either, and that I'm looking forward to learning how to run big whitewater. It takes them a moment to realize I'm joking; they are confused, disoriented, defensive, nervous, shy. I wish I could still experience the river with their freshness, though at different moments I am still all of these things, too.

After they've fidgeted through a few essential safety talks, and chosen a boat to climb into, for all practical purposes it's too late to go back; they've made the essential leap necessary for big changes; they've assumed all the inherent risk. It's much like in the sport of rappelling when you must finally stutter that first backward step over the edge of a precipice, live up to your commitment, and just GO. Pioneers must have felt this way a hundred years ago, leaving the safety of the known and heading beyond it. Though a river trip on the Salmon is not exactly uncharted territory, the emotional strain may be no less daunting.

And in some ways, neither is the terrain ahead any different—at least for these folks—than the frontier that awaited pioneers a century ago as they headed out of Independence, Missouri or Omaha, striking out for what was to them the great wilderness of the West. Though thousands of others have already passed safely down the river before these folks, in the same way that all but the earliest pioneers on the Oregon Trail followed others before them, it's still a frontier to each individual confronting it for the first time.

In 1893, the historian Frederick Jackson Turner delivered a lecture before the American Historical Association at the Chicago World's Fair, in which he posited that the western frontier stood out as the most important element of our history—both as a nation, and as individuals. He suggested that much of what we think of as distinctly American grew out of the availability of wild, untrammeled western lands where we could test ourselves and let our spirits run free. Democracy, rugged individualism, self-reliance, and many other characteristics commonly attributed to Americans, Turner proclaimed, were products of the frontier. Although his interpretation was meant as serious academic history, it huddled 'round the same fire as the growing mythology of the American West.

At the same time that he exalted the virtues and powerful influence of our seemingly endless, unexplored continent, Turner also concluded that the American frontier had irrevocably closed. He based this assertion at least partly on information from the U.S. Census Bureau, which defined the frontier as an area containing, on average, fewer than two residents per square mile. Robert Porter, the Superintendent of the Centennial Census, wrote, "Up to and including 1880, the country had a frontier of settlement, but at the present the unsettled area has been so broken into by isolated bodies of settlement that there can hardly be said to be a frontier line. In the discussion of its extent, its westward movement, etc., it can not, therefore, any longer have a place in the census report."

In the century since Turner announced that the most important epoch of American history—the frontier—had ended, his thesis has inspired and outraged legions of subsequent historians. By saddling up on that thin backbone between history and mythology, Turner created an ongoing theoretical shoot-out among various scholars whose own theories run the gamut from suggesting that the frontier promoted the antithesis of democracy and freedom and individualism, to the notion that American history has been in large degree the history of cities. And the gunfire hasn't stopped yet.

Part of the trouble may be due to the fact that Turner's thesis shares a few important aspects in common with the myth of the American West, which grew up alongside and out of his theories. For starters, both present a limited view of what occurred on the American frontier—a view that excludes most experiences other than those of "studly" white men migrating from East to West. They overlook the realities of Native Americans, blacks, women, Hispanics, Chinese laborers who reached the Pacific coast from the opposite direction, and even men who were weak, or unlucky, or who failed. These multitudes enjoy no place in Turner's writing, nor are they an acceptable part of the myth.

Turnerism and the western myth also both describe an idealized West that encompasses and nurtures rugged individualism, democracy, self-reliance and other admirable characteristics, but excludes the equally real traits of violence, lawlessness, nepotism, discrimination, cruelty, and other negative values that simultaneously characterized the West.

On the other hand, in a couple of places Turner's ideas diverge from the myth. One difference between them is a matter of degree: the myth romanticizes the West even more than Turner did. But the major point of divergence occurs where Turner claims that the opportunity to confront the western frontier that formed us as a people and as individuals, that was responsible for forging our uniquely American characteristics, and that challenged and inspired us to great ends, was no longer accessible as of 1890. Turner regrettably claimed that the frontier epoch was already behind us. The frontier had closed. The myth, however, fully relies upon the notion that a perennial frontier still and always exists somewhere out West. The myth assures us that even in our current state of overcrowding in this country, lonely, open places still await us beyond the next ridge, that we can pack up and head out to a territory where we can test ourselves, live freely, and develop the admirable traits of the frontiersman.

My season guiding on the River of No Return seems to have disproved the historian and supported the myth, or at least the part of the myth that suggests that the frontier—both geographical and personal—is still out there. The summer also made it clear to me that without the opportunity to confront a western sort of frontier in places like the Salmon River country, or in other wilderness, there can be no myth, and we would be poorer and far less hopeful without it.

In 1993, approximately one hundred years after Turner instigated this raucous and ongoing brawl among historians about the nature and current status of the frontier, the writer Dayton Duncan set out on a journey across the United States using the Census Bureau's definition of the frontier—fewer than two residents per square mile—as his map and compass. In *Miles From Nowhere*, Duncan wrote of this statistic as guiding principle, "It seems not just an abstraction, but an incomprehensible abstraction in modern times. It is Los Angeles County, the nation's most populous, with 8000 people instead of 8,863,164; Chicago's Cook County with 1900 residents rather than 5.1 million; all five boroughs of New York City with 600 inhabitants. It is 15,648 people spread across the state of Massachusetts. It is 6 million people in all of the Lower 48 states—the population of Indiana spread from Atlantic to Pacific, Mexican border to Canadian."

In spite of the unlikely survival of the frontier in light of these statistics, Duncan discovered that the 1990 census identified 132 counties in fifteen western states in the Lower 48 that still contained fewer than two people per square mile. According to the historical statistical definition of the frontier—which a century ago provided for the conclusion that the frontier period was over; and at a time when the myth of the American West has grown not only hugely popular, but simultaneously controversial and immeasurably important—Duncan determined that this essential part of our cultural history is in fact alive, if not particularly well.

Duncan also happened to mention that Idaho's Salmon River winds its way through one of these counties located along the contemporary frontier.

Even if the Salmon River country can be called a by-the-book frontier, commercial river trips through the area necessarily offer a tamer, diluted version of the now-mythologized frontier experience. But although signing on with a professional outfitter may minimize some of the challenges, it also makes the experience accessible to folks who are unlikely to buy the gear, obtain the expertise, and take off into the wilderness on their own. Commercial trips make it possible for many folks to confront the only version of a wilderness frontier they're ever likely to encounter, and thereby test themselves with some degree of assured safety.

Wilderness itself (a frontier requirement) has become rare and inaccessible for most people in the late twentieth century. In 1900, only five out of ten Americans lived in cities, but by 1980, the figure was nine out of ten. For a lot of urban dwellers who come to Idaho for a river trip, the Salmon still represents the outer limits: they may never have traveled so far from a road, or out of telephone contact before. A float trip down the River of No Return inspires that same wagon-train sense of moving across potentially dangerous and unknown terrain while relying on more experienced guides to assure their safe passage and to interpret along the way.

Many of our guests, I think, are drawn to the Salmon at least in part by this notion of the western frontier. They wish to see the kind of territory where homesteaders and gold miners and other western archetypes eked out a living in the wilderness; they want to experience the exhilaration of floating into that same kind of wild terrain, even though they're aware that it was mostly tamed a long time ago, and that they've chosen an easy route.

But what river passengers actually discover when scouting a dangerous rapid, or climbing into an inflatable kayak, or taking a ten-mile hike to the top of some distant ridge, or just by sitting around a camp fire in the evening with a group of people and no distractions beside their own stories and ideas, is that a week-long trip on the Salmon River presents them with many unexpected personal challenges. Historians may argue until the cowboys come home, but river passengers know personally how and where the frontier survives.

Over the past century, writers and scholars focusing on the American West have made a common and consistent mistake in trying to define and locate the elusive frontier: they've categorized it as a physical place that can be quantified with statistics or circled on a map. They seem to have overlooked evidence which suggests that the frontier is personal, as many of our guests come to learn. Despite facts and myths and numbers of residents per square mile, and at a time when few geographical locations are still wild enough to present uncharted terrain, the frontier that matters most to most people resides within.

It just so happens that wilderness, by offering a place where folks can escape the inane distractions and hypnotizing noise of contemporary society, provides people with a chance to hear other, more important voices that come from inside. Which is one of many reasons that we should fight as if our lives were at stake to protect the little wild country, and the few wild rivers, left to us.

While there seems to be a correlation between outer wilderness and personal frontiers, visits to this inner territory may assume many different forms and occur in a wide variety of locales. The frontier may also be a moment: when people confront the unknown, whatever that might be—a trek into the Atlas Mountains of Morocco; a double-diamond ski run in British Columbia; falling in love; undertaking their first session in therapy, or on a computer; or the instant when they step onto a boat at Corn Creek in spite of being afraid of the water and everything else that may lie ahead.

When I've finally convinced a couple of passengers to ride with me from the put-in for the first part of their seven-day Salmon River journey, and they've clamored up and sat stiffly in the bow of my boat, I often make as if to push them off and wave good-bye—as if I'm staying on shore and not really going along. That would actually constitute the best thing we could do for our guests, though it's not exactly practical from a business point of view. Because if these soft city folks had to jump behind the oars and row through rapids, unpin their boats from rocks, care for each other, administer first aid, and figure out how to cook their own meals beside the river, they'd have the very best possible and most genuine frontier experience. Such a trip would induce them to excel, and introduce them to aspects of themselves they might never have envisioned. As their guides, we know that the more actively they participate on this journey, the more likely they'll discover something, be struck by revelation, or undergo a transformative moment out there on their own frontiers.

As we push off from shore and drift out into the Salmon's current and head round that first bend—toward Killum and Gunbarrel Rapids just downstream, toward our first night's camp at Blackadar Beach, toward a week full of unknown occurrences—personal challenges will unfurl before us the way the frontier line once swept across the continent toward the West. Leaving Corn Creek, we're headed in that same direction. And even if we've been down the Salmon a hundred times before, there's no telling, on this particular trip, what kind of new territory we might encounter.

Water

"Who hears the rippling of rivers will not utterly despair of anything."
HENRY DAVID THOREAU

River. Stream. Creek. Runnel.

Rill. Rivulet. Brook. Burn.

Water—running, flowing, streaming, pouring, surging, rushing, murmuring, splashing, spilling, cascading, and meandering.

Swim, soak, wade, bathe, plunge, dive, and dip.

Sip, drink, guzzle, chug, quaff, and gulp.

Even water words, the language of water, purvey a quenching liquidity. Wa-ter. A fluid mantra. Wa...ter... Wa...ter... Deep, clear and deep. It sheds all meaning until only the sound and feel remain. Float down through the music of it, lose yourself and go under: patter of drizzle on broad leaves; hail dinking on tin roof; droplets leaping from spout to rain barrel—bloop bloop.

Oceans swell and surge, curl and break, and hearts beat to the percussive rhythm: whoosh...whoosh...BOOM...whoosh... whoosh...BOOM. Lakes reflect tranquil silence: ommmmm; ommmmm. Falls plunge into pools, snowflakes scuff ponds, rivers run into rivers—water upon water, water into water. The writer Raymond Carver called it "where water meets other water." Convergences, from mountain storms to prairie creeks to mighty rivers, all sliding toward the sea. A convocation of waters.

There is something, especially, about rivers. Alive with change at every moment, yet constant in their hypnotic redundancy. Shhhh. Shhhh. Shhhh. Veins of the topography, the beating pulse of the land. Seen from above the blue planet, like the intricate webbing of a leaf, the vascular architecture of a hand. We cannot escape metaphors for waters because water itself is too large and encompassing to grasp. It slips through the fingers. Yet we are immersed, drenched, soaked, permeated by waters. Rivers are earth in flux, alive, something to fear and worry about and love with great awe. Like the writer Norman Maclean, we are all haunted by waters.

And not just rivers themselves, but their intimate dance with beach, bank, and bedrock, slope and curve, carving channels through sandstone, limestone, granite, basalt; and the vagaries that incite and inspire rivers to rise in glassy green humps, to flood, to curl back upon themselves in milky green froth and pour over boulders, to rise in swollen brown muscular threat, to bubble, to drop clear and opaque from steep shelves, feathering whitely in free-fall, careening down rocky cascades. Endless variations, endlessly enticing. Infinite as the molecules that compose them, thundering to the edges of continents, and spilling over.

A flood of feeling. If only we could interpret rivers' messages. If only we could read the waters. If only we could ride the undercurrents to the end, and slide into a sea of emotion, headwaters of our humanity. If only we could give ourselves over to the flow and let it truly move us.

Whitewater

"It is no disgrace to be scared... In fact I wish to say that the person who is not afraid at certain places in the Salmon River has not sense enough to be afraid. I have met rapids before—shot them and poled over them—but never anything like the rapids of this river, and he who makes the trip can assert with truth that he has taken the wildest boat ride in America."
CAROLYN LOCKHART, NOVELIST, 1911

"It was easy. I expected the whitewater to be more challenging or more continuous. Like that whole Slide Rapid thing, when everybody was freaking out; I think I was right that it wasn't that big of a deal. Before, I thought that I must be really river-naive not to get nervous and that I just hadn't seen a lot of dangerous stuff. But now I've been around here a whole season and I haven't seen any river conditions that scared me."
TRISTA PATTERSON, RIVER GUIDE, 1995

One of the scariest runs I've ever had in whitewater occurred in the last half hour of my very first Main Salmon trip, which I guided for a college, where I worked in Portland, Oregon, ten years ago. My two passengers and I had just enjoyed a rollicking ride through Chittam and Vinegar Rapids, and according to my river map, we had approximately two miles to the take-out, with no more rapids to speak of. After we emerged from the giant waves in Vinegar, I irresponsibly removed my life jacket and we floated without a care on the cool green river beneath the blazing sun. I was happy to have made it safely through a challenging week-long run, and I surrendered to a kind of western reverie that hearkened back to my childhood, when for me the West was still an unrealized dream. We fell far behind our other boats, and I reveled in the solitude, all fear of whitewater having dissipated in the warm, dry air.

That is, until I happened to look down river and noticed a rapid called Carey Falls, which my *River of No Return* book describes as "sound and fury signifying nothing." But at very low water—such as we experienced on that trip—an almost invisible hole formed just downstream of a protruding boulder in the right center of the river. A hole occurs when water flowing over a rock displaces the flatter water on the surface just downstream of the rock, and then water just downstream of the hole flows back to fill in the space. A keeper hole is a deep and extreme version of this hydraulic, and one that forms so tight a circle of flowing water that it might spin an object—or person—indefinitely. Boaters refer to this circumstance as "getting Maytagged."

As we swung around the corner above Carey Falls, the other boats in our group had already run the rapid and floated several hundred yards downstream, and I had no idea which route they'd taken. I began rowing on the inside left, but when it proved too shallow, I changed course and pulled hard for the right side. I barely managed to straighten my boat out, and had lost all downstream momentum when I dropped over a slick boulder and into a hole that from above looked like little more than a harmless riffle.

And yet it stopped my fourteen-foot, fully-loaded raft dead, the way a brick wall stops Wile E. Coyote in a Road Runner cartoon. Stopped it, held it, and began torquing and lifting until the raft rose up completely on its side, dumping my passengers into the river. Then the boat slammed back flat before rearing backward like a bucking stallion.

As the raft climbed and twisted beneath me, I managed to haul my passengers back in. But the hole held us fast and dragged the raft back beneath the pouroff, which filled it with water up to the tops of the tubes. Gear actually floated inside the boat above my submerged legs. I cranked back on the oars with all my weight and strength, but each time I nearly pulled out of the hydraulic, the rapid sucked us back in. Downstream, the rest of our boats disappeared around a bend.

After about ten minutes of working us like a yo-yo, the rapid spun us at a new angle, sucked us in, and then simply spit us into the current. Floating freely again we bailed several hundred gallons of water and tried to collect the gear that had drifted out over the tubes of the raft. Kurt Wald, a young, Class V California guide who often seems to speak his very own language, would surely have called this "a yard sale." But with two swimmers in the hole and me without a life jacket, and our potential rescuers already far downstream, it could have been far worse.

More than forty rapids pepper the Main Salmon River in the seventy-nine miles between the put-in at Corn Creek and the take-out just beyond the Wind River Pack Bridge. The river drops 969 feet over that distance: an average of twelve feet per mile. But these numbers are deceptive because the gradient varies widely. The Salmon is a pool-and-drop river, consisting of long flat stretches interspersed with rapids that tumble precipitously all at once. The more formidable of the Main's top forty include Killum, Gunbarrel, Rainier, Lantz, Devil's Teeth, Little Devil's Teeth, Salmon Falls, Hancock, Bailey, Five Mile, Split Rock, Big Mallard, Elkhorn, Growler, Whiplash, Ludwig, T-Bone, Dried Meat, Chittam, Vinegar, and Carey Falls.

Below the Main Salmon, the Road and Lower Gorge sections of the river stretch for approximately another 113 miles to the take out at Heller Bar on the Snake. But while these stretches are often less scenic and intimate than the Main, they feature some gorgeous, narrow canyons full of very challenging—sometimes cranky—whitewater, including such Class II–Class IV rapids as Ruby, Lake Creek, Chair, Trap, Fiddle, Blackhawk, Roller Coaster, Green Canyon, Wright Way, Demon's Drop, Pine Bar, Packers Creek, Cougar Canyon, Cliff, Pipeline, Lorna's Lulu, Bunghole, Lower Bunghole, Harm's Hole, Bodacious Bounce, Half and Half, The Gobbler, Snow Hole, China, Eagle Creek, China Creek, Skeleton Creek, Wapshilla, Flynn Creek, The Slide, H-Hole, Sluicebox, Checkerboard, Eye of the Needle, Salmon River Falls, China Garden, Shovel Falls, Wild Goose, and Deer Head.

At different water levels, and depending on who's leading the trip, we may scout more than half a dozen of the rapids, or none at all. Scouting involves tying our boats to shore upstream of a rapid, and walking down to have a closer look at the whitewater so as to determine, at that particular flow, where the best route lies. In the least case, if we don't scout a rapid, we'll line up carefully and follow each other in—as I should have done at Carey Falls.

During one extremely low-water trip on the Main a few years back, we not only scouted almost a dozen rapids, but we were forced to walk passengers around several because the runs were so tight that the dories—made of wood, fiberglass, and aluminum—needed to be as light as possible to avoid smashing up on rocks. In contrast, this summer, I ran one early trip on which we didn't even scout the Main's major Class IIIs and Class IVs—like Salmon Falls, Big Mallard, and Elkhorn—because high water had mostly washed out the rapids, we were slightly behind schedule, and all the guides felt pretty confident of the runs.

Scouting not only allows us to see where we're headed and to form a plan; it provides time for us to take a deep breath, pay our respects, repeat our private river mantras and prayers, and gear up for the run—a sort of pregame ritual. But scouting also ratchets up the drama a notch or two. Don Litton (known as D.L.), a long time dory guide and son of Martin Litton, who originally founded two now-famous river companies (Northwest Dories and Grand Canyon Dories), feels that the very act of scouting imbues any run with implied danger. "I could scout some riffle and think: 'Well, if we have to scout it, there must be something to worry about,'" D.L. says.

But regardless of how many or which rapids we scout, the Salmon's whitewater provides no shortage of opportunities for mistakes, mishaps, accidents, bad luck, bad karma, and pure stupidity. Every summer we witness or experience all varieties of near misses in crafts of every kind. On a trip for thirty Boy Scouts this season, at certain times we had more than a dozen boats plying the water—including dories, oar rafts, paddle boats, inflatable kayaks (also called "Tahitis" after a particular model), and Revolutions (sort of like two hard-shell sea kayaks lashed together). And although we had a safety boater paddling a hard-shell kayak for making rescues, he seemed far more interested in surfing big waves than in guiding the scouts through the safest runs. So in several rapids, he led them straight into large holes, and kids were flipping and swimming everywhere—a total yard sale.

Although most adult passengers tirelessly scout rapids before running them in the inflatables, and they reassure us that they know the route, they occasionally botch it completely. On bad days they're forced to go for harrowing swims, or a hole spins them like laundry for thirty seconds, or they bang their helmeted heads on rocks.

Even boatmen occasionally blow the runs and float over holes, pouroffs, and sharp rocks, or careen into boulders, or slam into cliff walls, or get bounced out of their boats. I very nearly flipped a gear raft this summer on a gigantic rock that stuck at least six feet out of the river just above Myers Creek Camp, because I was enjoying a moment of solitude and singing an old Eagles song to myself rather loudly, and not paying attention to what lay ahead. Only one person—soft-spoken guide Robert Henry—happened to witness my error, and he was sensitive enough to keep this to himself.

We're never happy about running whitewater badly, but we do accept this as part of the territory. Talking about his major wall slam in The Slide Rapid at high water early this season, nineteen-year dory veteran Joel Mensik (grinning sheepishly and shaking his head) described it this way: "It was exciting. The folks I had in my boat didn't know how close I was to making it too exciting. I scared the ever-loving daylights out of myself, and they didn't even have a clue what was going on. I dodged so many bullets up there, but the river gods were extremely kind to me. I should have crashed and bashed a few times.

"I didn't weep about my run, but I wasn't happy with it. But I was happier than hell to be through there on the last day of a seventeen-day trip when we were looking at a rapid that could beat the crap out of us and we were the first boat of the season to go through. We were going through the unknown and that was a neat feeling. But I wasn't real enthused about that water level. It could've been the weather, too. It just had an ominous feeling. I had an eighty-year old man and a guy who didn't know up from down in my boat. And I had one good high-sider [someone who throws his weight on the high side of a boat, if necessary, to keep it from flipping] who saved my butt."

I had plenty of chances to relate to Joel's feelings about bad runs. Even when you get through okay, it's sort of like doinking a tennis shot off the handle of your racquet and still winning the point. You know—and so do any other boatmen who caught you—that you blew it. And you know they know, and they know that you know they know. And so on.

Of course, we all make an occasional mistake in whitewater yet nearly always squeak through without harm. The worst part of running whitewater clumsily is that it causes people who don't know better to underestimate the power and threat of the river, and to lose respect for rapids.

One year during low water we spent a long time scouting Bailey Rapid (named for Robert G. Bailey, who wrote the original *River of No Return*) and planning a route through the very tight rock garden along the right side. I'd carefully plotted what I thought was the best run. On the water, my moves were crisp and efficient, and I executed every stroke I'd intended, but I miscalculated the power of the current, which flowed directly toward a dome of rock that I meant to slip just left of. In the last frantic seconds before crashing into the domer, I pivoted my boat and pulled back two strokes against the river and my own momentum, but the boat hardly responded. My bow barely kissed the dome, but the impact spun me so that I bounced sideways through the final drop, careened right and then left out of control, and popped into calmer water through no fault of my own. It wasn't a terrible run, but I was disheartened and disappointed in myself. Still, my passengers cheered wildly, perhaps thinking I'd intended these thrills for their enjoyment.

And though such runs sometimes suggest that you'd have to

be both really lame and genuinely unlucky to get seriously hurt or killed on the Salmon, that's just not true. But this attitude leads many private floaters to perform unbelievably stupid acts—such as drinking beer all day while simultaneously running whitewater; or floating without a map; or, as I saw once on the Deschutes River in Central Oregon, hand-paddling through the Class III+ Oak Springs Rapid on an inflatable alligator.

Regardless of how it might seem, whitewater is dangerous and without sympathy—especially if you treat it casually. People get killed on rivers all the time, not in any trendy, adventurous, exhilarating way but really, actually dead. Even flat water claims its victims. Carrey and Conley's *River of No Return* offers dozens of examples…

In 1890, when the Wet Gulch ferry capsized on the Lower Salmon, twenty-five cows drowned. In 1915, Gene Churchill, who wore a prosthetic arm, was riding in a boat that wrecked on a rock near Richardson Creek. When friends tried to pull him ashore with ropes, his arm harness broke. Churchill couldn't swim. His body didn't surface for nearly a month. A year later, Dolly Cain's two brothers both drowned when they swam across the river to visit her on Christmas Day. In 1920, Maude Howard died by a sand bar in front of her house when she went into the river to rescue her niece, who'd experienced some trouble while swimming. The niece escaped unharmed. Jack Ranger decided to swim the river instead of walking the distance to his friend's boat one day in 1925, but he never made it across. In 1935, Anthony March wrecked a boat in Salmon Falls and dove after his bedroll, but never needed it again. Another boater wrecked his craft in Big Mallard Rapid, and barely escaped from the craft when his pants caught on a nail. In 1962, Lucky McKenna was driving a jet-boat up Dried Meat Rapid when he lost power, and a wave broke over the boat and pushed it into a hole. In spite of his name, McKenna, his mother, and three children drowned. A professional river guide flipped a boat in Vinegar Rapid in 1976, and though passengers swore they'd spotted him climbing out of the river on the right bank, he was never seen again.

This season alone, I heard of two people drowning on the Salmon. One man tried to cross the river at high water in an open canoe and was swept downstream. Later in the summer, a familiar Salmon character named Eric, who worked as caretaker at several properties along the river over the years, drowned after jumping off the Campbell's Ferry Pack Bridge without a life jacket in July.

People who pay attention to such stories, who watch a stick buffeted by the current or swept under a rock, people who are naturally cautious, know how dangerous whitewater can be. In talking to some of the older Dory guides about whitewater, I was sobered by the degree of respect they still have even for small rapids they've run a hundred times without mishap. Many guides confessed that running whitewater makes them plenty nervous.

Lonnie Hutson—known as "the Master" to some younger guides—told me what's most frightening is that "with certain rapids at certain water levels, you can do everything perfectly and the outcome is still not predictable. I don't care if I've run The Slide fifty times at 29,000 cfs [cubic feet per second]; I'd probably be just as amped. We ran it with three dories at that level this year and one guide had the best and smoothest run, except that he flipped. I still get adrenaline rushes at high and low water."

Some guides who've grown a little casual running whitewater create new challenges for themselves to help maintain their edge. At first they may aspire simply to get through a particular rapid. But once they've accomplished this they may raise the stakes by intending to get through without even dinging a rock, or by executing the minimal number of strokes, or by pursuing a more challenging route.

My heart still grows deliciously fat with adrenaline nearly every time I float toward a riffle of whitewater. I feel a mixture of fear of serious bodily harm or personal failure, responsibility for my passengers and gear, and the kind of electrical charge you get when you start down an advanced ski run, or step up to the plate in baseball with men on base and the game on the line—a kind of performance rush, a hyped-up feeling of spontaneity and abandon. It makes me want to yodel, to row hard, hit the biggest waves, and bellow nonsense syllables—ay ay ay eee haaw—as loud as I can.

I would like to see the historian Frederick Jackson Turner row a raft full of trusting passengers through The Slide at flood stage, or make the low-water run at Elkhorn Rapid in a fragile wooden dory, and then tell me that the frontier closed a hundred years ago.

The Dories

"The best of it for Rudi, he says when asked to sum up the whole thing, was living on the boat all those years...you sleep on them, you brush your teeth in them, you go off to work in them every single day. It's been a wonderfully simple life, to live in a beautiful place, on a lovely little boat, surrounded by the best of friends."
LEW STEIGER, RIVER GUIDE, IN *THERE'S THIS RIVER*, EDITED BY CHRISTA SADLER

"The dory ride itself is so much fun; you get much more out of the waves, instead of just slopping through them, like you would in a raft. And the dories are truly beautiful. As a photographer, after shooting dories it's hard to even point my camera at a raft. Rafts are like store-bought corporate tomatoes, compared to dories, which are more flavorful and fresh off the vine."
LEON WERDINGER, RIVER GUIDE

In the late afternoon we pull our two dories—The Morro Rock and The Lake Tahoe—and one big, ugly, yellow gear raft up on the sloping, sandy beach of a no-name camp. The dories look sleek and streamlined tucked in the small eddy, sterns nosing up toward the brown, grassy hills above us. They look even more attractive parked next to the cluttered gear raft—which resembles the truck driven by the Beverly Hillbillies—because the dories carry supplies neatly packed into hatches hidden below the flat, gleaming decks.

The day is hot and dry now after raining in the morning, and suddenly seems made for swimming, so after unloading gear and setting up our kitchen we do just that. When we guides have immersed ourselves in the cool green water, and checked in on the guests—who are reading and napping in the shade under a copse of trees—trip leader Kurt Wald calls a formal crew meeting on his boat. We round up our Dories mugs as Kurt pulls ice and fresh limes and tonic water and a bottle of Gilbey's out of his left side hatch. It's been another great, long, tiring day on the Lower Salmon. This morning we floated through the steep narrows of Cougar Canyon, and ran some rowdy whitewater. In my dory the ride felt boisterous and spirited; I hit the waves aggressively and smiled just to have this gorgeous, lively craft under me. I pushed hard on the oars and my heart soared. We emerged from the rapids and shadows of Snow Hole Canyon in the early afternoon, into the first warm sunshine we'd seen in days.

Now, we unwind in grand repose on Kurt's boat, with the river nuzzling persistently against the bow where it juts out into the water. We sip icy cocktails, leaning back against life jackets we've laid out to cushion the gunwales. The day is done: we've put in our hard work, brought boats and passengers safely down river again, and all is well. We savor this moment of respite, and drink to how lucky we are to live in the world—especially to live in it as dory boatmen.

As we taste the cold, bitter sweetness of gin, we tell stories, as river guides sometimes do at the end of the day—outlandish, woeful, half-believable tales about passengers bringing blow dryers on trips, and ex-guides running whitewater with buckets over their heads, about moose and rattlesnakes in camp, and bears on golf courses, stories about sprightly boats, and bad runs, and fearsome rapids—while the sun creeps slowly overhead without making a single demand. We luxuriate in this hour of free time before the dinner crew must begin marinating the chicken and baking the spice cake for tonight's dessert.

Kicking back on the boats like this—on the dories—was a welcome occurrence throughout the summer. We would never have bothered to gather on the clumsy tubes and messy decks of a raft. But once we've pulled the dories up on shore and they've ceased to function as boats, they still look far too pretty, far too welcoming to ignore. We are always drawn back to them, whether to sip cocktails, or share a can of Pringles or some other treasure pilfered from the hors d'oeuvres bucket, or to slug morning coffee and talk about the rapids ahead, or doctor an injury, or sew up a torn pair of Tevas, or eat our dinners in peace. The boats serve as bar, cafe, living room, back porch, and office; I attended several "official" crew meetings aboard dories this summer during which every agenda item was a Miller Genuine Draft.

On some rare afternoons, if I wasn't leading a hike or tossing horse shoes with a guest or helping someone with some piece of uncooperative gear, I napped on a pad spread across a dory deck in the warm sun—still on the water, still aboard, but with nowhere to go. In the fiery depths of August, I occasionally rigged one of the giant striped lunch umbrellas on my own dory and leaned back in cool shade against seat pads, put my feet up, drank a soda, and wrote in my journal for an hour before firing up the stoves to start cooking. Or invited another guide over to talk. Whatever we needed we could find inside the dory: sleeping bag for a chilly evening, first aid kit, river map, cold drink. Pop a hatch and there it was. We'd hunker like children on a self-contained sofa island in the wide, calm river of childhood. And all around us, the prettiest scenery you could ever hope to see.

Many dory guides even go so far as to sleep on their boats at night. In bad weather, after drinking too much and forgetting to pitch his tent, one guide slept inside his boat, down in a damp, stale hatch that smelled of the melons he'd been carrying for five days. Most guides also spend hours attending to their boats, washing them down, waxing the oarlocks, tinkering with every detail of care and feeding. Barry Dow, one of the surviving old-time "codger" guides, who used to wear only a loin cloth all week and occasionally pitched kitchen utensils into the river if they failed to work properly, could sponge sand off his decks all day long. If a passenger tracked a speck of dust onto his boat, Barry would continue to act professionally, but you could see utter disdain in his tight, thin-lipped grimace. Once I watched a very smart little girl dare to carry out what dozens of trainees had undoubtedly wished to do to Barry many times over the years, in response to his ornery behavior: she poured a bucket full of sand into his stern hatch. Barry spent the next forty-five minutes upside down in the hatch sponging out every last grain.

There is definitely something different—something nearly sacred—about the dories, something which gets at exactly who we are and what we're doing out here on the Salmon River, and on the Colorado, and in other places where guides row these improbable boats.

Dories are handmade out of wood, fiberglass, and/or aluminum, and at our company we hand-paint them in turquoise, red, and white. Each dory has a name, an individual character, a set of special oars meant for that boat and painted with a design that matches the mural painted on the flat rear transom, as well as matching the decoration of the boat, itself. Rowing a dory, you develop a relationship like the bond a cowboy forms with his horse.

Running whitewater in a dory, the ride is dangerous and stirring, the animal itself full of strength and fragility at the same time. It seems to breathe beneath you as you talk it through rapids. These boats come alive in whitewater, as if they're actually ecstatic to be there. They practically sing. In some less dangerous rapids, we encourage passengers to bow ride—to climb right up and straddle the very front tip of the boat and hang on like bronc busters as we seesaw through big waves. The boats pitch and buck with the spirit of the river, filling your heart with riotous pleasure. What a neat idea that someone thought to build these craft to travel on the water, on rivers, with a kind of rambunctious grace and style.

For at least a few guides—especially those of us who read a lot of Edward Abbey—the Glen Canyon represents the ultimate dory to row. This elegant wooden boat features a mural painted on the transom, of a dory riding a giant cresting wave through a crack in the Glen Canyon Dam, the structure that backed up the Colorado River and buried one of the earth's most beautiful places under 300 feet of water so that people who shouldn't have been living in desert places like Phoenix and Las Vegas to begin with could run their air conditioners more cheaply and water their lawns. The mural implies that the river will eventually win out, even if it requires a little help from a boatman with a knowledge of explosives.

Wooden dories, in particular, also connect us to the earliest river runners—not only sweep-boat captains on the Salmon in the nineteenth century, but explorers such as Major John Wesley Powell, who first traveled the Colorado River in 1869 in wooden boats. These western pioneers adventured down uncharted rivers long before the advent of dams, when you never knew what awaited around the next bend; when the West was still largely *terra incognita*, and the very names of western places—Lolo Pass, Gospel Hump, Missoula, the Idaho Territories—conjured images of boundless freedom and adventure. For some of us they still do.

Much of the Dories mystique is also based on the confidence and skill and self-reliance of dory boatmen. Whereas rafts can slide sideways over ledges, and bump and spin off rocks, the dories broadcast a resounding "kaboom" through the canyon when they hit an obstacle. Which not only identifies the guilty boatman, but can also punch a hole in his craft, requiring hours of repair and self-recrimination. In the dories, executing a clean, perfect run is as important as planning a sensible route. We aspire to excellence, and then must live up to our expectations.

This whole dory thing began back in the 1960s with a man named Martin Litton—a writer, outspoken conservationist, and Sierra Club executive board member; a man of passion, vision, and stubbornness, with a deep honey-roasted voice and a reputation for flipping boats. Litton led a dory trip through Marble Canyon on the Colorado in an effort to fight the dams the government planned to build there. He also founded Grand Canyon Dories and Northwest Dories, and was the first to run these boats on commercial river trips.

Telling "Martin stories" has become a sort of sport among guides who worked for him in the early years. One of my favorites describes how Martin flipped a dory in Lava Falls on the Colorado River, one of the largest rapids in the world. Supposedly, while he was in the middle of a nasty swim and gasping for air between huge, muddy, breaking waves, a rubber raft pulled up beside Martin and tried to rescue him. But he refused to climb aboard, saying he would rather drown than ride in a raft.

According to many of the folks who worked for him, Martin was not in business to make a lot of money; he founded the Dories as a way of enticing more people to fall in love with the canyons so that they might work to defend wilderness. Litton's unwavering notion of what was important, his unyielding determination to do things the good way, the right way, defined his river companies. The dory boats themselves were visible manifestations of his vision. Litton named each of the boats after what he called "environmental sins." Read together, these names form an elegy: Glen Canyon, Copper Ledge, Malibu, Tenaya, Peace River, Clearwater, Little North Fork, Quartz Creek, Chattahoochee, Nile Delta, Hetch Hetchy, Diamond Head—hauntingly beautiful, once-wild places destroyed by the solipsistic, short-sighted plans of men.

Many of the guides drawn to work for the Dories were equally passionate and idealistic. They shared a vision of wilderness adventure as spiritual journey, and rowed for Martin because they admired him and believed in the same things he did. They were pioneers who figured their way through difficult rapids in these fragile crafts by flipping, smashing up, and even sinking boats in those early years—part of the Dories legacy, the price of exploring along an unknown frontier. Don Litton (D.L.), Martin's son, told me about how during a particularly high-water year, two guides refused to row through Crystal Rapid on the Colorado because they saw no way of getting through it upright. Martin grew determined to row all three boats, and he flipped every one.

The dories were always more than just beautiful boats that provided a titillating ride. They became a symbol of excellence without compromise, an exquisite, powerful craft that required special skill and handling that you had to develop and earn. Rowing a dory isn't like driving a Rolls Royce down Hollywood Boulevard in L.A., which anyone with money could do; it's more like driving a Ferrari on the mountain roads of Italy, something not advisable until you've acquired the proper abilities and an appropriate respect.

These days, however, you're as likely to encounter a dory parked in the tall grass in the field out behind Boatland—O.A.R.S.-Dories' headquarters in Lewiston, Idaho—as you are to see it on the river. When Martin sold Grand Canyon Dories and Northwest Dories a few years back, Curt Chang, the Idaho Area Manager, bought the Idaho-based branch with his wife and her brother. But when their marriage broke up, so did the business partnership. They sold the operation to George Wendt, owner of O.A.R.S., a large California-based rafting company that had no experience with dories. Possibly when O.A.R.S. realized that dories are more expensive to operate than rafts because they require constant repair and are difficult to transport, the company replaced dories with rafts on many trips. Also, lacking Martin Litton's vision and focusing more on the bottom line, O.A.R.S. just didn't seem to comprehend the Dories mystique, the Dories magic. In spite of their service record, history, aesthetics, and great ride, and in spite of the fact that guests love dories, the boats languished out behind Boatland, on their way to becoming an endangered species.

Of course, there may be another logical side to this, and George Wendt might very well possess figures that explain why beaching the dories made good business sense. But to guides and passengers who've floated a western river in one of these boats, no explanation will do.

It always saddens me to come upon dories on dry land when I'm in town between trips. Although I've only rowed a couple myself, the boats are like old friends you run into unexpectedly after a long while—friends you've spent intimate times with, teammates from your sporting days whom you come upon as they're spectating from the stands; seeing them, you feel sympathy and a slight twisting in your heart. You wish them good things and hope to spend more hours with them some time soon.

These boats are so important to us that many Dories guides aren't willing to work for just another rafting company. Rowing rafts after you've earned a place as a Dories guide would be like working as a dude wrangler—running fat city folks around a fenced ring on tired nags—after riding the open range and breathing the scent of sage on the wind.

As guide Brannon Riceci told me, "To those of us who started with the Dories, a rafter is a dirty guy who flies a pirate flag—the total unprofessional slacker seventies throwback dude—and we don't want anything to do with that. Any time we talk to somebody and they ask what do we do, we say we're whitewater guides. None of us say we're rafters.

"But then people say, 'Oh, I have a cousin who does that on the Deschutes River. Is it like that?'

"At first I was like, 'No, it's nothing like that. It's in Idaho, on a real river—there's no road, there's no train, we're not in a rubber raft. We're in a dory.'

"But now I say it's exactly like that. Now I'm a whitewater rafting guide. Everyone knows a guide. It's not that big a deal to be a guide. It's not that big a deal to have done anything anymore. Everyone's done everything. Now you can't have summited Mount Everest without someone telling you about someone they knew who was in base camp when the weather really howled. Everyone's got their story. You can't impress anyone anymore.

"Still, the dories are the one thing that sets us apart. There are 5500 licensed guides in Idaho, but only about fifty people who row dories. That's important, and we all deal with a lot just to row those dories."

Some of our guests this season had no idea what a dory was, and they were surprised to see these imposing boats on their "rafting" trips. O.A.R.S. reservationists (now called "adventure consultants") often failed even to mention the dory option to many customers.

And at first a lot of passengers avoid these mysterious crafts. They've heard of whitewater rafting, and look forward to bragging to their friends back home about how exciting their rafting trip was. They have no reference point for dories, and they may fear losing prestige by having to explain about these other boats to folks who know even less than they do. But once passengers grow comfortable and eventually bored with their rafts, and they climb aboard a dory, we often can't get anyone to ride in the rafts again. Guests love the dories' clean decks, the unrestrained rides, the slick runs full of daring, danger, and finesse. They feel exhilarated knowing their guides have to do things right—one good bonk against a rock makes this very clear. And they doubtless notice how we revere the dories. They see us sleep and eat and drink on the boats, and they want to be a part of this special dory thing, too.

If, as a company, we're truly dedicated to the business of experiential adventure; if we really care about providing the most wonderful and unique river experience; if we want to be better than a hundred other river outfitters who run cushy, generic trips on dozens of western rivers, the dories make us special—and most dory fans would say the boats are a big part of what makes us better, too. Whether dories continue to ply the waters of the Salmon, to float regally down stream among dozens of clumsy rubber rafts, or whether they'll go the way of other extinct species—and whether Dories guides will go that way, too—depends partly upon whether vision or profit motivate the company in future years. And there's a good argument that says O.A.R.S. could successfully focus on both simultaneously, because the Dories vision and mystique are quintessentially marketable.

For me, dories are about pride and purity and individualism: there's nothing like rowing past a group of rafters and having them stare admiringly and a little jealously at our boats, nothing like running rapids well when you know that the consequences for mistakes are large. But for me dories also come with a hatch full of fears and responsibilities. When Curt Chang scheduled me for a twelve-day dory trip at the beginning of August, it was only the second time I'd had my own dory on a trip. I felt honored and nervous as hell. Curt warned me to have clean runs, as if maybe I'd had it in mind to go out and bash up the boat just for fun.

My dory, the Morro Rock—named after a spot just off the California coast where a nuclear power plant was built—looked to have been parked out behind Boatland for quite some time since its last river voyage. But I grudgingly fell in love with the boat despite its tired appearance. Pure white on the outside, and sporting a turquoise deck with red highlights, the Morro was designed to ride high in the front, and heavy. When other guides asked what boat I'd be rowing, and I told them, they always responded: "Oh, the Morro Pig." It was not the choicest of assignments, but it was mine and I swore to be true to it.

For the first four days of the trip I rowed everything perfectly, amazed by the boat's responsiveness compared to a raft, the way it practically danced over waves, white bow angling up toward the denim sky. Approaching rapids, I stood in my footwell and scouted the surface for every rock, overcompensating to miss each one by half the width of the river. I was working too hard, but could feel myself becoming a better, more responsive boatman.

On day four, in Five Mile Rapid, I experienced my first hit. A week earlier I'd run a raft right over the top of a pourover six feet from the left bank, where the entire pushy current flowed. This week, in the dory, the run was just to the right of the hole. As I floated down and aimed for the slot between hole and shore, I noticed that the hole had actually become a huge boulder as the water level had dropped, so I pushed away from it just a little too hard and banged the bottom of my bow into another rock jutting out from shore. The hit sounded like a rifle shot, and jolted my passengers up front.

It was really only a minor ding, but I was scandalized. I felt as if I'd just let a baby carriage roll out into traffic. This priceless boat had been entrusted to my care and I'd proven myself unworthy of the responsibility. Full of self-loathing, I looked at my passengers, Bob and Vera, a couple who wore matching tee shirts every day of the trip. They alone knew my secret, but I figured maybe they'd be happy to have a story to tell the folks back home: how the rapids had been so dangerous that their guide crashed into a wall just to avoid a killer hole. I also figured maybe that was a story I'd have to embellish for Curt Chang when I returned home to Boatland and he asked about the damage to the boat, and when I was planning to repair it.

That afternoon, when we pulled into camp, I emptied my

hatch on the side where the hit occurred—removing buckets full of food, the fire pan, cans of beer and pop, a drink cooler, and a bag full of charcoal—and sponged two inches of water out of the bottom of the boat. But when I mentioned this to Kurt Wald he said he'd been bilge-pumping gallons of water out of his boat every afternoon, and he hadn't hit a thing. Still, I felt as if the boat knew I'd mistreated it, so I sponged it out every day for the rest of the trip.

Two days later we seemed to be getting along quite well again. I'd taken to washing down the decks after breakfast—until they sparkled—as a form of penance. One morning, just after I'd finished, Vera climbed aboard for the day's ride and tracked muddy shoe prints from bow to stern. When she noticed the dirt, she said, "You know, Kurt keeps his boat spotless. Maybe I should ride with him."

During the rest of our journey, I scraped the Morro lightly two more times and experienced one more real hit—in a rocky rapid named Blackhawk. In spite of these lapses, I felt a strange intimacy develop between the boat and me, something I can't quite describe. For all the time guides spend talking about their dories, this relationship remains just beyond the realm of explanation. If you've never felt a powerful attachment to a boat, any account of the feeling will sound childish or just plain bizarre.

How can I amply describe something which is sleek vehicle and safe refuge, dependable partner and object of obsession, symbol of all that is good and free and pure and unrestrained, yet moody, demanding, and vulnerable? How can I communicate the look another guide throws you if you bump his dory or scrape its side with your oar? How explain that moment of sheer terror and regret, when a boatman cocks his ear to an impossibly minute sound and then sprints across burning sand and sharp basalt to interpose his body between his dory and shore because he's heard a jet boat approaching, and realized that its wake might bang the delicate curving side of the boat into the rocks along the river bank?

Guides

"The American cowboy has come to symbolize freedom, individualism, and a closeness to nature which for most of us has become a mere mirage; hence they serve as a safety valve for our culture."
MARSHALL FISHWICK

"River guiding is a cowboy sort of job. You're always sleeping outside and cooking outside and living on the shores of the river. A lot of people say, 'Are you nuts? What are you thinking?' But a lot of other people are really envious. A river takes you back to your primeval status. Sometimes the further you regress, the happier you are. Guides are at the bottom of the food chain and proud of it."
KURT WALD, RIVER GUIDE

"Guides are generally people who don't accept things as they are, they question things rather than accepting the typical American lifestyle. Guides make conscious choices for themselves as to what's important, and what they want."
PETE GROSS, RIVER GUIDE

"The river has always been a haven for misfits"
CHANA COX, *A RIVER WENT OUT OF EDEN*

When we pull into Rhett Creek Camp—a lovely spot with tall shade trees and a meadow full of purple and white sweet pea flowers, and a beach that slopes gently down toward a wide, still eddy—two of our passengers and one guide are not feeling well. All three were on the Middle Fork trip that preceded this one on the Main Salmon, and they are not the first group of folks from that trip to fall ill. At Rhett, we begin referring to this day-long sickness as "The Middle Fork Crud," and Rhett Creek earns the nickname "Retch Creek."

As soon as we've tended to our ailing comrades and set up the kitchen beneath towering Ponderosa pines, and the other guests have gone off to the meadow to pitch their tents, I notice Joel boiling up large pots of dishwater, though it's early afternoon, hours before dinner.

Although nobody has asked him to, and he hasn't mentioned his intentions to anybody else, or conferred with us, or requested help, Joel spends two hours thoroughly washing every dish, cup, fork, spoon, and spatula on the trip. When I ask what he's up to, he says that with so many folks getting sick it just seemed like a good idea.

A few days later, on the Lower Salmon portion of this same trip, an elderly man experiences some problems with infected fingers. Twice daily—after breakfast, and before dinner—Joel boils up clean water and soaks the man's fingers before wrapping them carefully with clean gauze. He never complains or asks anyone else to assume this responsibility. He just sees what needs to be done and takes care of it—not because he has to, but because it's the right thing to do, and because he cares.

In spite of an acute tendency toward crankiness, and occasional bouts of screaming at trainees or grumbling about who-knows-what, Joel often acts like the consummate boatman. His moods may swing between moroseness and a sort of giddy, cornball goofiness, but on many occasions Joel is not only incredibly likable, but demonstrates the exact kind of selfless hard work that we should all aspire to.

Another moment comes to mind when I think about guides acting transcendently professional under duress. My last trip of the season featured one of the most difficult collections of clients I've ever encountered. Two families of very rich Chicagoans came on the river with more special dietary demands than a band of diabetic kosher vegan Muslims on a Jenny Craig program during Ramadan. Although they snacked on chocolate bars and potato chips and candy all day, and brought their own beef salamis for us to slice up at lunch and serve with special mustards and other condiments, their group organizer insisted that we offer low-fat, low-sodium dinner options every night. So in addition to preparing, for example, two huge vegetable lasagnas from scratch, garlic bread, a giant and multifaceted salad, and fresh-baked apple crisp for two dozen people, we also had to fry up garden burgers and boil chicken hot dogs and prepare some plain pasta—with and without sauce—on the side. While we worked in a great frenzy to pull all of this together simultaneously and present it prettily on a table decorated with flowers and pine cones, members of these families would wander into the kitchen and pick food right off the prep tables and eat with their hands.

I was standing with Andy Persio, a mellow young California guide, behind the serving table on a particularly tough evening late in this trip. In the course of about thirty seconds, four different people complained about the meal we'd been working on for the past two hours.

Why couldn't we make little mini pizzas for dinner?

The salad dressing was too oily.

They'd just finished a snack and weren't hungry yet.

Could we possibly slice up some more salami and put that out with some kind of delicious bread?

Andy was keeping an eye on the pot of coffee that we had to brew each night with the trip leader's special coffee beans so that he could drink one cup (with skim milk), when somebody else came over and asked if maybe we could brew a pot of decaf, too—how could we expect them to drink regular coffee at eight o'clock in the evening, did we want them to be up all night, they'd specifically requested blah blah blah...

A knife rested on the prep table next to where Andy stood, and I saw him consider it for just a little too long as his face grew flushed. But then he turned to me and made the strangest sounds—"co co coo coo kee pee co pa?" Then he turned back to the guest and made the same monkey noises again, and the look on his face was weird enough to make her sidle away from the table and forget all about her freshly brewed decaf.

Andy and I stood quietly for a few moments before I turned to him and asked, "What was that?"

"Purge valve," he said, referring to the mechanism on a raft that allows excess air to escape from the inflatable floor so that it doesn't explode.

For me, this is the hardest part of guiding: doing everything for everyone all day long—sometimes as if they are incapable of caring for themselves. Yet doing it with kindness and understanding and not a speck of resentment. It's being "on" like this for sixteen hours a day that presents a boatman's greatest challenge. Among other things, being on includes maintaining a positive, professional, and friendly attitude when you've dropped an eight-pound Dutch oven on your foot, or someone wakes you up at three A.M. to help him put up the tent you offered to help him put up at four P.M. because it looked like it might rain that night. Or when you've spent half an hour tying bags down to a gear raft and somebody wants to fetch his Chapstick out of the one on the bottom—and this same thing happens every day.

Most passengers are a delight to travel with, and getting to know them is one of the true pleasures of guiding. But nearly every trip includes one or two who will push our buttons and test our limits and remind us that guiding is still a job.

Brannon once told me a story about how he'd reacted in a less than textbook manner under similarly challenging conditions.

"We were trying to close up the kitchen one night after dinner, so we kept yelling last call on dish water, last call on dessert, last call on this, last call on that. But people kept coming up to me to solve problems that were so basic, like 'The zipper on my jacket is broken.'

"'Okay,' I said, 'I'll fix it.' It's not like I'm a zipper expert, but I had the initiative to sit down and work it out. Finally I stood up on my boat and screamed, 'Last call on any crew service!' I got a letter about that one.

"The way to stay happy as a guide is you've got to cut the people some slack. That's so hard after you've been here a while and everything is so easy and you know where everything goes. It's so obvious that after you wash your dish it goes in the dish bag; if you don't know that, you're stupid.

"But these people may come from a place where they've never washed their own dish in their life, they may never even have seen a dish being washed. Sometimes you have to deal with them as if they're children, and you have to do it in a non-condescending way. You have to explain things to them on a very basic level and accept that as soon as you finish talking to them three of twenty-four will come up and ask verbatim the questions you just answered. So you make a game out of it and just laugh, and you say you're laughing because you're a happy guy, and you just answer the question. Otherwise you'll rip their heads off. There's no other way around it; as a guide you have to learn ultimate patience. If you give them the benefit of the doubt, they really appreciate it by the end because they realize how dumb they were."

Guides must possess a wide variety of personality characteristics and special skills. As Kurt Wald says, "A good guide is somebody who can put the needs of everybody else before his own, and can relate to people and massage their attitudes and do whatever it takes. He can talk to a five year old kid on that level and turn around and talk to somebody who's a biophysicist. Certain guides have a knack for that that never ceases to amaze me."

All of which is to say, simply, that being a river guide—especially a Dories guide—involves far more than steering a boat down river through a bunch of rapids. In fact, most boatmen would agree that running whitewater is the easiest part of the job. The real challenge involves serving as camp counselor and confessor, family therapist and naturalist, teacher and parent, cook and rule maker, fun monger and safety officer. A guide not only has to change roles and attitudes to suit the mood of the moment—instigating a game when everyone's depressed about the weather, or motivating folks to help with pack-up when they're tired from a morning hike but we're already behind schedule; he also has to juggle these roles in such a way as to get through to people of widely varying expectations, personality types, experience, and style. And guides have to discover the appropriate way to push people to challenge themselves in the outdoors—the thing that will absolutely make or break their trip—without crossing a vague and dangerous line.

Today, the world offers few opportunities for men and women to live lives full of adventure and individualism along unknown frontiers. In the latter part of the twentieth century, working as a river guide presents a simplified modern version of the same challenges; guides have inherited the legacy of ruggedness and self-reliance once attributed to mountain men and pioneers.

Frederick Jackson Turner could have been talking about river guides when he described "...[t]hat coarseness and strength combined with acuteness and inquisitiveness; that practical, inventive turn of mind, quick to find expedients; that masterful grasp of material things, lacking in the artistic but powerful to effect great ends; that restless, nervous energy; that dominant individualism, working for good and for evil, and withal that buoyancy and exuberance which comes with freedom—these are the traits of the frontier, or traits called out elsewhere because of the existence of the frontier."

Though most would never be so self-absorbed as to see themselves in this light, river guides are the rightful heirs to the mythology of the American West. They are nearly as much a part of the myth as were the very first river explorers, or the scouts who led other Americans West into a more encompassing and wilder frontier a century ago.

I can say this because, while nearly one of them, I also stand apart—as a writer, as an Easterner, as a man who lives their life part-time, which is hardly better than not living it at all. Because to truly engender that western spirit is to give yourself over completely to such a life, to let go of everything else and live for the living, to cross the line and make tracks for the unknown. It's to live—as my friend and fellow guide Leon did—in a truck for seven years, driving from river season to river season, from the Rio Grande and the San Juan to the Salmon and the Snake; to hole up in the constricting winter season with someone you love at least for a while—preferably someone with a caretaking job and a wood stove—until snowmelt fills the rivers with whitewater in the spring and the whole thing starts again. Such wildness is not a choice so much as an instinct, the same kind that propelled explorers farther and farther West, the kind upon which the American myth was constructed. I recognize the tendency to over-romanticize my colleagues, but that, too, is part of the legacy of the mythological West.

The men and women who guide river trips are lucky enough to spend many of their evenings in deserts and forests, surrounded by mountains, under skies that crackle and blink with stars. They watch improbable sunsets. They cook high-carbohydrate dinners as shadows purple the river canyons and reflect off the water in evanescent hues. Sometimes, in the mornings, guides plunge into the cold river to wake themselves from sleep. They spend occasional afternoons with their boats wedged on rocks in the middle of swift currents, wishing they'd looked a little more carefully at their intended routes. They work hard. They play old Grateful Dead tunes on battered guitars and eat a lot of rice and beans. They also care deeply about the earth, and about wilderness. They are hard-nosed, independent, and often hard to reach. They are part of what little remains of the mythic American West—part cowboy, part pioneer, part mountain man and woman—and they are an endangered species, threatened by dams and forest clear-cutting, by their very isolation, by technology and economics and other forces that intrude upon a simple and pristine way of life. Their lifestyles are now as tenuous as were those of the first mountain trappers, whose era abruptly ended when Europeans no longer favored beaver hats.

River guides are quirky, individualistic, a little crazy, and often as various and wild as the rivers they run. The best guides are experienced (don't refer to them, in person, as "old codgers"), they're natural leaders, and they can teach you about history, geology, weather, astronomy, and other aspects of river travel. But they can also take a group of total strangers and make them feel like honored guests at the greatest floating party ever thrown. They are part shaman, part professor, part game show host, and part professional athlete, and the good ones are as passionate about their work as anyone you're likely to meet.

Many guides also have other important skills: some are teachers during the year, and so may have great rapport with kids. Some are writers, craftsmen, artists, musicians, scholars, or storytellers. Regardless of what they are, or do, they have the ultimate power to inspire, protect, entertain, and enlighten you in just seven days on the river. Cherish them: they are a dying breed.

Guides are also as different from each other as the various types of folks who pioneered the early West. As much as they have in common, they are also unique, uncategorizable, impossible to generalize about. There are the codgers—old-time boatmen like Barry and Joel, who know every river story, who can explain each nuance of rapids, flora, and fauna, but who may grow moody without warning and retreat into themselves. There are the young, quiet, hippyish guides, gentle and soft-spoken and truly funny when you make the effort to listen to them—Eric and Max, Matt and Robert. There are the natural leaders, like Bronco and Rondo, and the trainees—many of whom were women this year: Trista, Sandra, Rebecca, and Sky—making the same dumb mistakes we all made, working their butts off, paying their dues and turning assuredly into great guides.

O.A.R.S.-Dories guides encompass people like Kurt Wald, who's committed to rafting and fishing his way through college, and graduate students such as Remony and Sandra, and people like David Sears—college professors with Ph.D.s. There's Lonnie—the guide's guide—smooth and slick in every way; and Chris Quinn, who forgot nearly all our essential gear on a trip late in the season but made the passengers laugh their asses off for a week. There's Leon, who focuses so much energy on developing great interpersonal dynamics, as often as possible through games.

Once you have an idea of who guides are—that the group as a whole is characterized by creativity, high energy, good looks, individualism, humor, and a surprisingly high level of education; and that as individuals they scatter across a wide spectrum—the natural question to consider is: why have they ended up as river guides when it seems like they could do anything.

For starters, doing most things might actually require getting a job—a word that may scare some guides from the room. The point of many of their lives seems to be pursuing what they're passionate about, what excites them, what seems important, and spending their time and energy in activities that are personally rewarding and a whole lot of fun. Also, some guides feel as if they don't quite fit into normal American society; living outside along the river provides a comfortable place where they can at least partly hide from the real world and avoid all the aspects of it that seem so ludicrous. Many guides also work on the river because it's their way of contributing to the good of the planet; if they can inspire even a few passengers each summer to join an environmental organization, or fight to protect a place, or even if they can just make a couple of folks feel something out there, they believe they've accomplished as much as can be expected of a person. And, of course, guides work out there because they love the river; it compels them.

These days, as pressures increase and the wilderness becomes more crowded; as trips focus more on service and less on experience, turning guides into glorified, if less well-groomed, flight attendants; and as some newer guides seem more concerned with money and whitewater thrills than protecting beautiful places and helping people have moving experiences in them, some guides are beginning to look elsewhere for the things they once got from running river trips in the American West. They're floating rivers in South America or Nepal, maybe, or taking up sea kayak guiding, or quitting outdoor recreation altogether so as not to have to watch their lives on the river become mainstream and corporatized.

As Frederick Jackson Turner described the metaphorical precursors of river guides, "...the over-mountain men grew more and more independent. The East took a narrow view of American advance, and nearly lost these men."

Today, we may lose them still.

An Anthropology of Boatland

"Only persons of independent disposition, of great initiative, and impatient of government control were likely... to emigrate to the colonies."
WILLIAM A. MCDOUGALL

By the end of the summer, the following statistics had been preserved in blue-green marking pen in a corner of the message board in the commons room at Boatland, our headquarters in Lewiston:

6/23	39k
7/3	34k
7/24	11k
8/6	8k
8/10	8k
8/14	Rickshaws-R-Us

The numbers to the right of the dates represent river flow readings in thousands of cubic feet per second—the volume of water rolling past the Whitebird gauge downstream of the take-out for the Main Salmon. The readings appear a bit haphazard because they weren't written at specific or consistent intervals, more as if some guide sitting around Boatland sought a way of feeling connected to the river when he wasn't out on it, and phoned to check the flows. Like when city folks call to hear the snow report at their favorite ski mountain, and take comfort in knowing what the weather is like in some distant place that they love and hope to visit soon.

The final reading for August 14th implies that although June featured record high flows, two months later the river had dropped low enough to make you wish you could drag your boat behind you on a couple of wheels. For the weeks remaining in the season after mid-August, nobody even bothered to update the numbers, probably figuring that water levels would continue dropping until you wouldn't even want to know—especially if you were scheduled to a row a dory on a late-season trip.

Still, stories reside in these numbers: tales about dangerous high-water runs at The Slide Rapid, and how the murky river eventually ran green; about dories banging rocks later in the summer, and passengers high-siding, and big horn sheep wandering down on hot days to drink; about lyrical moments of adventure and discovery, challenge and running from challenge, and a thousand other details hidden in implication. Stories of what the river was like, and what happened on it, and what it had to say at various times and flows.

If the Salmon River itself presents a sort of modern frontier, then Boatland constitutes our wilderness outpost, our colony perched on the tamer side of that frontier. It's a safe place from which to monitor conditions beyond familiar terrain; the place to which we return to rest and resupply and prepare ourselves for another expedition into the wilderness, where our hearts remain. Boatland is our Rendezvous—much like the sites where old fur trappers gathered between forays into the mountains, a predetermined location where we greet old friends and tell stories and share meals and talk about the places we've been and what occurred out there in the wild: how a guide parked his dory on a rock in Elkhorn Rapid, or five Boy Scouts paddled inflatable kayaks into the hole at Ludwig, or someone slept with somebody they weren't supposed to. Boatland is not quite set amidst the civilized world (you'd agree if you saw the kitchen), but doesn't quite reside in the wilderness, either. Out behind the building, guides park the campers and pickups they live in, or out of, between trips, like mountain men setting up their private camps in a wide meadow where others like themselves have gathered for a few days respite.

And if Boatland is a sort of wild western territory, an outpost set on the edge of the vast Idaho wilderness, then Curt Chang—O.A.R.S.-Dories' Northwest Area Manager—is our law. Inevitably as you wander around this small, bustling country trying to find something or somebody, Curt will find you first, with some kind of job for you to do. Since he is solely responsible for scheduling guides on trips, you never tell Curt you don't have the time to help move a dory, or put something out in the shed, or run an errand. He is a man of few words, and the kind of boss with whom you never have any idea where you stand. When I inevitably ask him during trip pack-up where I might find the portable showers, or a vegetable peeler, or a seat pad, he rolls his eyes up toward the high ceiling, swipes at his forehead to push back a strand of hair that isn't there, and utters those few words that he is a man of: "C'mon c'mon *C'MON!*" Sometimes when he speaks, his sentences dive into silence, as if shot down in a vapor trail of syllables that leave you guessing at the rest of what he meant to say.

And yet, even while he's often as uncommunicative as a western sheriff, Curt gets the job done, maintains a semblance of order, and attends to an incomprehensible number of details and logistics. Considered by virtually all boatmen to be a fantastic guide, he now spends most of his time in town—the lawman's equivalent of a desk job—trying to run this part of the company and at the same time keep Boatland peaceful, if not exactly squeaky clean.

The actual term "Boatland" usually refers to the entire complex at O.A.R.S.-Dories headquarters in Lewiston, which consists of several offices and a combination meeting room/store (selling tee-shirts, books, river gear)/supply area (housing turquoise dry bags; rain gear; red, blue, and yellow sleeping pads; white ammo cans; and tents in red, black, and purple bags) up front; a raft room full of rolled boats, metal frames, inflatable kayaks and paddles, air pumps, safety lines, and other assorted gear; a big, airy shop—smelling of Pine Sol, mildew, and toluene, and hung with racks of dory oars—where guides repair injured boats; a commissary lined with shelves full of trip food and dry goods, and giant freezers (Curt locks this room at night, but you can break in using a credit card or even a dollar bill if you need toilet paper or a half-empty box of Ritz crackers at one A.M.); a couple of small rooms stuffed with auto repair tools, first-aid supplies, and various other items of miscellaneous "schnadel," as many guides would say; a dark upper landing hung with orange life jackets; and the guides' quarters upstairs—three small bedrooms, one messy commons area (named "The Room of Doom," after a powerful, inescapable eddy beside a rapid in the Grand Canyon), and a truly scary, nearly third-world bathroom. The dories themselves live out back, with some of the guides.

The upstairs guides' quarters at Boatland look very much like a temporary encampment. The Room of Doom—where we attend pre-trip pack-up meetings and often hunt and gather in the refrigerator for old trip food we'd be willing to eat (and guides are not choosy)—has collected the kind of desperate, broken furniture that folks might have abandoned beside the rugged trail West: a vinyl couch with only one arm, and that one is broken; two woolly orange chairs with suspicious stains; one black Naugahide easy chair with ripped upholstery; and an old school desk with attached seat that only the tiniest guide could squeeze into. Neighborhood kids wouldn't even drag this stuff back from the dump to furnish their clubhouse up some tree. These items appear so tired and ugly and battered that they inspire disdain rather than sympathy.

Between the seating places, a couple of coffee tables hold old *Outside* and *Paddler* magazines and Patagonia catalogues, James Michner novels and cheap mysteries without covers, books about the river, and letters from various environmental groups begging for contributions. Empty wine bottles and ratty socks and decrepit hats, dry bags and life jackets and personalized ammo cans with thermal Dories mugs hanging on by climbing carabiners, and various other gear litter the floor. Gathered together, these artifacts define our summers; added detail upon detail, they compose the stories of our lives.

Above the ailing couch, guides have decorated a cork board with recent trip photos. The earliest shot from this season depicts an upside-down snow-covered raft that got away at the put-in for the first Middle Fork trip in June. There's Brannon rowing a boat occupied by three beautiful young women suntanning in micro bikinis; Curt Chang with a weird smile on his face, apparently demonstrating some game you play with a quarter; a close-up of Leon with a goofy grin; Robert Henry wearing a Hawaiian lei. All the usual suspects.

On the opposite wall, behind one of the orange chairs and next to a broken aluminum dory bow that somebody has hung—evidence of some classic boatman blunder—and just above and behind the wood stove, the colorful magic-marker message board seems constantly to remind Ed to call Jano, and Kurt Wald to call his mother, and for the other guides to perform their chores, and for someone to go see Curt. It announces a special 'Friends and Family Trip' on the Middle Fork in September, and that Idaho Rivers United tee-shirts are on sale in the office downstairs. It assigns pack-up crews for specific trips, and often communicates messages that almost no one can decipher. These are our pictographs and petroglyphs. They explain our history. They, also, tell the stories of our summer. High on the walls above these, someone has painted red and turquoise dory stripes, as if the commons room is a giant boat upon which we're voyaging together.

On the kitchen side of the room—where the greasy orange carpet gives onto grey linoleum—most traffic flows past the fridge leaning against one wall. Guides have adorned this barrel-chested model with bumper stickers that read: "Fix The Dams; Free the Sockeye" and "I'd Rather Vacation at Suncrest Motel, Salmon Idaho." Leon also stuck a kitchen magnet to the fridge that he created out of a photo of Brannon wearing a pink dress and black irrigation boots and a long blond wig, and jumping high in the air with his legs akimbo.

Next to the fridge, in the center of the kitchen area, sits a solid, blocky, scarred table that could survive a nuclear war, surrounded by a ragtag assemblage of wounded chairs. On the wall across from the hulking fridge stand a stove, a sink with cupboards and drawers, and an ancient microwave. In the sink you're likely to exhume the cast-iron skillet, plates and mugs, and science experiments that survive as the only evidence of various improvised meals. The mailbox/cubbyholes with each guide's name, as well as a pay phone with a cord that's just short enough to prevent you from sitting down at the table beneath it—and on which whispered conversations in the crowded room either preserved or ended many long-distant romances—adorn the wall perpendicular to the fridge.

Throughout the summer, I noticed different guides sitting at the kitchen table and eating their peanut butter sandwiches or their jack-cheese quesadillas and reading the very same weeks-old copy of *USA Today*. I picked up and read several different sections on three or four occasions in the course of three different months myself. Between trips we hunger for news of any sort, for even the remotest connection to the world, even if that connection is no longer current. It's as if we've been away for so long that any information will fascinate us—much like the way western pioneers probably welcomed the slightest communication from the civilized society they'd left behind.

These items and messages and patterns of behavior constitute a boatman anthropology. To study the clues at Boatland—to peek into the three bedrooms and the bathroom off the commons area; to look behind the tacky seventies-era silk-screen of a sailboat hung in the bathroom above the commode and see where an old guide punched a hole in the wall after losing his job; to watch us greet each other and plan our days off and grumble about schedules or management—is to read the undercurrents of a river season, and river lives.

And yet, in spite of their sad evanescence and the impermanence of the clues we leave behind; in spite of the pathetic furnishings and slap-dash character of everything in Boatland; in spite of the fact that we live there between trips to the river, where we really wish to be, I still love these rooms. They exude the comforting scent of warm toast and dusty desert air and moldering fruit and anticipation. Everything about them communicates the message that you'll be leaving again, that tomorrow or the tomorrow after you'll set out on the green, clear river once more. Boatland is simply the place you stay before departing, where you see guides you haven't seen all summer, where postcards from passengers, and packages from home, and letters from lovers, and bottles of peppermint schnapps appear in your box; where at 5:30 A.M. before a long Main Salmon drive, some bleary-eyed misfit offers you freshly brewed espresso. Where, in the warm purple evenings we parade through these rooms wrapped in towels, fresh from the shower, hair glistening; or wearing jeans so worn they're almost white, and clean tee-shirts, as we primp for the post-trip dinners at Jonathan's Restaurant. Boatland evokes the nostalgia of summer camp, the promise of a college dorm, as Pete plays his guitar in a corner and you hear footfalls on the wooden stairs and always look up in anticipation. Finally, Boatland is nearly always about anticipation, about what comes next. We are all embarked upon a grand and wild adventure together, and the journey begins tomorrow. Or just ended yesterday. The present hardly exists at all.

For some reason, I've witnessed the most consistently beautiful sunsets I've ever seen from the second-floor stair railing behind the guides' quarters, or while sipping beer on the deck of a dory parked out back, or from the grass beside a pickup spilling trip gear as a boatman tries to organize his life. On most summer evenings, the sky out beyond Boatland fades to peach and lavender and tangerine. Guides are divided on what causes the warm, sprawling colors: some attribute it to pollution from the Potlatch pulp mill beside the Clearwater River that runs through downtown Lewiston. Others think it's the way Boatland perches high on the edge of steep hills that roll down toward the river before rising up in the heat beyond it on the other side, creating a valley expanse that absorbs and mutes the light before reflecting it back out into the wide distances.

But I think it's because we see something special, something subtle, something implicit in these western sunsets, something that reminds us of the wild lands that we're on the verge of, and will visit again soon. I think it's because we can feel in those sunsets the letting go of these attachments we call our lives—that letting go which must occur before we head out on the river one more time.

The Putting Out Before the Putting In

"I believe work is good for you. Unless you work pretty hard you'll never be healthy. If you can't discipline yourself, don't worry about your future. You don't have any."
SYLVAN HART, A.K.A. BUCKSKIN BILL, THE LAST OF THE MOUNTAIN MEN

We are working at the boat ramp at Corn Creek in the late afternoon, unloading all our trip gear off of a truck and trailer and distributing it among our five boats, when D.L. asks if anyone has seen the drop bags for the raft frames. The drop bags hang down from the frames, creating an enclosed space to pack a lot of gear into; without them, major sections of the frames are rendered as useless as a suitcase with no bottom.

After searching through our piles of gear we realize that we've forgotten the drop bags. So we send Marvin, our driver, back out the unpaved road twenty miles to the nearest telephone to call Curt Chang at Boatland. We're hoping that Curt can send a few extra drop bags from the town of Salmon with trip leader Chris Quinn when he drives the passengers in tomorrow morning. But shortly after the dust is settling back on the road from behind the departing truck, Andy Persio inquires as to whether anyone has seen the com (commissary) box, an item roughly the size and weight of an economy car, which contains virtually every essential item from our kitchen, and which Chris had so diligently and thoroughly packed up. When we deduce that the com box is probably still sitting out beside Boatland where Chris—an excellent if forgetful guide—had been filling it with gear, D.L. climbs into our other vehicle and takes off after Marvin, so they can relay both oversights to Curt Chang at the same time—not a happy task.

Unfortunately Curt can't scare up another com box, so after Chris finishes running the passenger orientation meeting in Salmon that evening, he climbs back into the van and drives five hours halfway back to Lewiston to rendezvous with another driver who travels the other five hours toward Salmon with our com box. Chris then motors five hours back to Salmon, arriving just in time to pick up the passengers in the morning to drive them to the put-in at Corn Creek. Having just met Chris the night before, they probably assume that he always looks haggard and worn out. When he arrives triumphantly at the boat ramp in the morning with the passengers and extra drop bags and the com box, we have no idea that he's also forgotten to pack any knives.

Chris actually runs an awesomely fun and excellent trip, and I only mention these events and poke fun at him because it could easily have been me—or any of us—who forgot such crucial items. But it wasn't: it was Chris.

As with any good mystery, the processes of packing and rigging for a trip always reveal some unexpected twist, such as which piece of essential gear we may have overlooked. These kinds of problems arise out of the complex logistics of gathering and packing gear at Boatland, driving it many hours to the put-in, and only then rigging our boats and noticing what's missing.

Packing and rigging often prove to be among the most challenging parts of river trips, especially to less-experienced guides like me: they create tremendous potential for screwing up. Completing these tasks successfully has always seemed as miraculous to me as running rapids safely.

We began pack-up for this particular trip, as usual, up in The Room of Doom at Boatland. Our crew gathered around on the ramshackle furniture while Chris distributed a list that included the names, heights, weights, and ages of our passengers, where they were from, and any special medical concerns or dietary restrictions we needed to know about.

Then, as Chris assigned specific gear loads to each guide, we scribbled notes on our trip lists. He also revealed his tentative game plan for the trip—where he wanted to camp, how he preferred to arrange cook crews, what kind of mood he wished to create—preferences which often bear little or no similarity to the way things actually unfold.

Then we were ready to go downstairs and confront our gear. Pack-up can take anywhere from two to nine hours, depending on the T.L.'s organizational skills, how many guests are on the trip, the determination and experience of the guides, and other circumstances beyond our control such as whether the food packers in the commissary have finished loading our coolers, and just how hungry we are. On this particular trip, we expected much of our gear to arrive later in the day, when another trip returned from the Middle Fork. So after rounding up what items we could, Chris and Andy Persio and I pursued the only logical option at that point in time: we bought a six-pack of good beer and went out to play golf.

The pack-up process itself—which we began in the early evening—is difficult to describe. Imagine four or five people participating in a complex scavenger hunt in a large building with many rooms connected by narrow doorways, trying to gather items as diverse as spoons and two-man tents, buckets and whiffle balls, tables, wet suits, cheese, and coffee pots. We ran from commissary to raft room to the shed out back, constantly in search of the single clipboard that listed all essential equipment, interrupting each other's quests to ask for help in lifting or finding some heavy or elusive item. We dashed past one another over and over again, mumbling to ourselves. Once we'd gathered all the gear in piles around Boatland, we drove a truck or trailer to each pile and packed it all on.

With luck, for most trips, we usually finish pack-up early enough to go out for the requisite red curry and swimming Rama at the Thai Taste Restaurant before returning home to Boatland in the hot evening to begin the adventure of sorting through and packing our own personal gear. But on this particular night we finished late enough to render dinner inappropriate.

The next morning we woke before six, stumbled down to the shuttle vehicles, and drove ten hours along the Clearwater and Lochsa Rivers, over Lolo Pass, through Darby and Hamilton, Montana, before turning west again toward the Salmon, and eventually following the dirt and gravel road from North Fork to the put-in.

When we arrived at Corn Creek in the late afternoon, I walked down the concrete boat ramp to the water to see what level the river was flowing at. For some reason, the Forest Service had cemented a pair of tennis shoes into the ramp when they built it, and you measured the water level here in feet above or below the shoes. On my first trip of the season, in June, the gauge read 7.1 feet above the shoes. The river roared past, muddy and threatening. By late August the water had dropped to .5 feet above the shoes—still higher than the highest reading for the previous summer, but by then the river had turned glassy, revealing the stones of its bed and flowing with a deep green serenity. A chart beside the ramp converts the sneaker measurements to cubic feet per second (cfs); boatmen employ both stats when describing river levels.

When I'd allowed myself this last moment of repose, and the other guides had unfolded themselves from the vehicles and stretched and yawned sufficiently to shake off the long drive, we started unloading all the gear and rigging our boats.

Just as the act of rowing boats on a free-flowing river expresses an inexplicable purity, the chaotic process of rigging boats also involves a sort of Zen-like beauty. The dories require far less labor to rig than do rafts. Although sliding the heavy dories off their trailers and into the water requires a team effort, once afloat they are "good to go," as Kurt Wald might say.

As soon as you know what you'll be carrying, and we've unloaded these items from the truck, you simply pack them in the sealable hatches below the dory decks, trying to balance the sides evenly. You don't even have to tie anything in; simply stow heavy items—bags of charcoal, propane tanks, fire pan, square white buckets full of wine or food—up front, and leave such items as a drink cooler, first aid kits, and lunch accessible. Beer and soft drinks fit right beneath the footwell where you rest your legs while rowing. Light bags full of clothes and other personal items fit in the rear cross hatch directly under and behind where you sit, or in the bow and stern hatches, where passengers will also place their ammo cans full of the gear they may want throughout the day.

The challenge is to balance your load, know where everything is, and not crush the melons. Packing a dory is like assembling a large jigsaw puzzle, but one that allows for creativity: a cubist jigsaw puzzle that can fit together in a variety of ways. Once loaded, the dories look sleek and spacious because everything lies hidden from sight below the decks, save for a rescue line, spare oar, seat cushions, and a couple of small bailing buckets. I've found that spreading a river map on the deck beside me makes for a nice aesthetic touch that passengers appreciate, in addition to helping me figure out at any given moment exactly where I am.

Rafts are another animal altogether, and unfortunately we were all rowing rafts on this trip. The requisite rigging, strapping, and cinching provided just one more reason to resent these crafts when perfectly capable dories were languishing high and dry in the field behind Boatland. We heaved the rafts off the truck like giant plastic jelly rolls. We opened them without ceremony or happy admiration, and inflated them to their full sixteen clumsy feet with an electric air pump that whined through its entire task.

When the rafts were firm we lugged them down to the water and fitted each with a series of metal frames that rest across the tubes, and which we strapped to the metal D-rings glued onto the outsides of the tubes. The main frame holds the oarlocks, and provides an anchor for hanging the wooden floor that serves as a deck in the center of the boat. This frame also provides a place to drop in a cooler—the boatman's rowing seat—by means of a couple of straps, in much the same way that graveyard workers lower a coffin into a grave. The front of the main frame contains a rectangular space where we would have hung a heavy canvas drop bag if we hadn't left them all in Lewiston. We would have hung another drop bag on a separate frame and attached it behind where the guide sits.

Let's pretend for a moment that we hadn't forgotten the drop bags (which Chris would bring with him the next morning). After hanging them on the frames, I continued rigging my boat by filling the rear bag with cases of beer and soda, a spare propane tank (which we call a bomb not because it might blow up—which it might—but because it's shaped like one), and six square, white, sealed buckets packed with and labeled: Wine; Dinner #3, Chicken Teriyaki; Dinner #4, Pesto Linguini; Dinner #5, Pork Tenderloin; Hors d'oeuvres; and All Breakfasts. Perishable items for these meals were already stashed in coolers. I stuffed extra spaces with loose items such as a shovel, tarps, or the extra filter for the water pump.

Next, I filled my front drop bag with five rocket boxes (rectangular waterproof metal boxes actually used by the military for carrying rockets) packed with garlic bread, eggs, glass bottles of condiments, and other food. Then dropped the produce cooler (a better choice than the dairy cooler, which contains such potentially spillable items as sour cream and milk), in its slot and cached a few beers down in the bottom. Closed the hinged metal drop bag lids, covered them with sleeping pads, and cinched them shut with straps. I left the front surface clear for passengers to sit on, and later built a pyramid of dry bags on the drop bag lid behind me and tied them in. Stuck two more rocket boxes filled with such items as cookies and bread on the hanging floor on each side of where my legs would rest; this is a crucial strategic maneuver—you want to choose rockets that will lose some of their contents early on so you can stow personal gear (rainwear, snacks, bottle of Cuervo for evening cocktails, Edward Abbey book) that you wish to have easily accessible in the extra space. Eventually I filled the space between my rear drop bag and the stern of my boat with such loose items as empty buckets, extra kayak paddles, an air pump, a day bag, and various other schnadel. When passengers actually boarded my boat, I'd strap their ammo cans to the flat part of the center frame that fit over my tubes.

There is an aspect of rigging rafts that's much like solving one of those logic puzzles on standardized tests where you've invited eight people to a dinner party and must arrange the seating, keeping in mind that X cannot sit next to Y, Z must face directly across from Q, and each guest must sit between two others of the opposite sex. Rigging requires intuitiveness, but until you really get it the whole process seems completely random and full of entropy. Becoming a good guide requires attaining a state of flow during rigging.

Most importantly, you must remember not to pack some item that you'll need for lunch in the bottom of a drop bag that you'll cover over with dry bags and intricately strap down. Such a location is particularly inappropriate for cookies, I learned early in the summer, on a Lower Gorge trip. Since you can't serve a lunch without cookies, I had to deconstruct half my over-killed rig job on a rescue mission to pull out two boxes of Chips Ahoys. It's not the Dory way to just let such a mistake slide. Knowing where all your gear is and even knowing for certain which items you're carrying—especially if they're small items like the minced garlic, or pesto sauce—is no easy task.

When we finished rigging—or at least as much as was possible without com box and drop bags—sometime in the early evening, and the light had grown soft over the river, and the air had cooled, and the other boaters had wandered off to their campsites to cook dinner, we rowed our crafts upstream to a beach where we could sleep close by them. We dined on cold pizza and cold beer. Just before dusk we were lucky enough to watch a resident moose swim across the river and snack on riparian vegetation not far from where we sat. The moose eventually sashayed right through camp and poked her bony head into our boats, as if inspecting our rig job, as if wondering how we could run a river trip without drop bags and a com box.

On most trips, if we'd rigged well, and our guests weren't expected to arrive until ten A.M., the night and morning were surprisingly leisurely. This trip was no different because we couldn't rig any further until Chris arrived with the rest of our stuff the next day.

When I woke just after eight, light ascended slowly above the ridge downriver, and somebody had already brewed a giant pot of cowboy coffee. We drank it slowly from our thermal Dories mugs and breakfasted on muffins and melon and cereal with milk, and attended to a few last minute details: lining up the orange life jackets on the blue tarp; pumping air into the inflatable kayaks; reading through the guide book to remind us of good stories that took place nearby; brushing our teeth—all as the river flowed ceaselessly past and we awaited the moment when at long, long last the passengers would arrive and the current would carry us downstream with it, toward limitless possibilities.

Passengers

"Appreciation of wilderness began in the cities. The literary gentleman wielding a pen, not the pioneer with his ax, made the first gesture of resistance against the strong currents of antipathy."
RODERICK NASH, *WILDERNESS AND THE AMERICAN MIND*

"My favorite passengers are East Coast city folks because they appreciate it more than any other group. All their preconceptions are changed, they get way excited by every little thing they see, every detail of camping, or the canyon, or rocks, or water. Some people have never sat and watched a river run for five minutes constantly and they can't believe it keeps going on and on. That just shocks them and they get inspired."
LONNIE HUTSON, RIVER GUIDE

"For passengers it's a cutting-edge adventure. I've seen them on the first night thinking, 'I don't know if I can take this.' Then all of a sudden they don't think twice about things. They change and accept things and you see their guard drop. They may not realize it on the river, but when they get home they realize they have experienced something really special and it has made them better people, given them more individuality, more self respect. It changes them and makes for a better life outside of the river. A lot of folks say it's the first time in twenty years they've been themselves. And it may be the only time."
JOEL MENSIK, RIVER GUIDE

Five of us have just finished de-rigging all the gear from a six-day Main Salmon trip and loading it into the back of a truck and onto trailers, and now we're bouncing down the gravel road in the crew cab on our way toward Riggins, and pavement, and, eventually, Lewiston. It's quiet at first, as dust flies off the tires and we exhale slowly and lean back in our seats with nothing to do but ride—our first moments of repose in over a week. But as we cruise along the river, and the rapids below the road draw our eyes irresistibly down to scout them, we can't resist another instinct, either: to talk about the passengers who drove away from the take-out only two hours ago, and with whom we just shared a very intense trip.

So we swap stories of strange things we witnessed: somebody sneaking out of someone else's tent just before dawn, a small flower tattooed on a middle-aged buttock, a conservative guest who seemed to be getting high every time he visited the unit (our portable toilet). We debate about whether a certain woman's breasts were really her own. We exchange secrets we've uncovered: that one family came on this trip the day after their daughter ran away from home for the third time. That a gentle old man lost two of his children in two different accidents. That the woman we'd nicknamed "Prozac Queen" just finished with a long, nasty divorce.

We're tired and cranky as the crew cab jostles over the rough road, and one boatman begins to rant about a guest who really pressed his buttons all week—reminding him a little too much of a particular family member he could never abide. When he finishes his tirade, he jokes that guiding river trips would be about the best job you could ever have if we could just get rid of the passengers.

Ah, the passengers, whom we love and disdain, admire and hold in contempt, for whom we feel deep affection, sympathy, admiration, embarrassment, frustration, hope, fear, resentment, confusion, and often pure amazement—that they could be so kind, so inept, so earnest and excited and open, so very naked out here in the wilderness; that they could appear to grow so much in such a short time; and that this river we've come to love in a familiar way could seem to them such a challenging and far-out frontier. Our guests are fun and spontaneous, repressed and overserious, straightlaced, enlightened, or just plain weird, and there is never any way of predicting what they will do or say or ask for or give. Every time we think we've figured them out, they'll perform some action that astounds us. Who could possibly know, at any moment, what in the world they're thinking?

And though all boatmen occasionally feel that our job would be better without them, the truth is that whether we adore or despise them, whether they're the most inspiring or the least aware, passengers provide one of the main reasons any of us venture out on the Salmon to begin with. Passengers allow us to live this western dream we've made of our lives. They are essential to our livelihood because they pay our salaries and provide the impetus for us to guide (there wouldn't be any outfitted river trips without passengers), but they are also important to each and every one of us in many other and far bigger ways.

Passengers constitute as major a part of guiding river trips as do running whitewater and exploring side canyons and sleeping under the stars. Most guides work out here because we're driven to share our love of the river and the feelings it elicits. We believe we've discovered one of the great secrets of the universe, and we're so caught up in our own passion for it we can't help but proselytize and emote. We are evangelical about wilderness; knowing that our guests might experience a new and unparalleled joy out here, we take them down river hoping to convert them. This whole thing is so good we just can't keep our mouths shut. We just can't keep it to ourselves.

Longtime guide Don Litton is especially articulate about how the river works its magic on folks. D.L. says, "I like to see other people have the experience of falling in love not just with this place, but with a place inside themselves that they don't have any other access to. They experience something out here that's of a spiritual nature. We're almost like missionaries trying to bring people that experience."

Of course, we're not so altruistic that there's not something in this for us, as well. D.L. goes on to add, "Most guides have had some kind of spiritual experience out here that they want to protect. They've fallen in love with the place and want to nurture it; they want other people to see it in the same way because they realize instinctively that to protect the experience and the place, other people are going to have to fall in love with it, too."

Many boatmen tolerate low pay, difficult work, long hours, and an indifferent corporate structure simply to have the chance to provide this type of experience for our uninitiated passengers. But at the same time that we're constantly putting out for them, passengers—in their own various ways—offer plenty back to us in return. Watching them open and change in the backcountry, and begin to love the wilderness is deeply gratifying. Seeing them react to the same frontier that originally brought many of us out here and changed us also reminds us of how far we've come.

If a wild river journey happens to constitute a kind of frontier for many of our passengers, the passengers themselves—more than the weather or the rapids or even the wilderness—make guiding a frontier experience for us. They create the tone, dynamic, and experience of a particular week on the river. They challenge and surprise us the way a frontier should, making every journey different even as we run the same rapids and cook the same pork tenderloin with new potatoes at Rhett Creek Camp on night three week after week. As Joel says, "For me, every trip is like the first trip because I've never gone down the river with these particular folks before. That keeps it exciting."

Watching passengers face their fears, spend time with their families, push their own limits, and interact with other folks also provides us with rare insights. Our greatest challenge on the river is to remain sensitive and open enough to understand what's going on for each guest, how we might move and excite them, when we should be gentle and reassuring, when we should challenge them to do something difficult, and what lessons they have to teach us—intentionally or inadvertently. Passengers constitute a wilderness that we have one week to explore, and if we're observant and kind, just watching them and interacting with them may reveal to us some of the great secrets of the backcountry of the spirit, the deep, uncharted territory of human nature.

Passengers begin to teach me things the moment they show up at the put-in and I form initial impressions that almost always prove to be wrong. Just when I thought I'd pegged a guest named Glen as a redneck, he shocked me by reciting poetry from memory around the fire one night—not just Robert Service, but Frost and Longfellow, sonnets and love poems. When I first got a look at a couple named Tom and Corrine at Corn Creek, I guessed that they were a kind of biker pair who'd ventured out of their element. For starters, they were shy in a way that suggested they wanted to hold themselves apart from the group. Tom was burly and a little threatening with his wild beard and silent manner. Corrine seemed tough and a bit abrupt. It took me nearly two days to learn that they were both hard-working, highly-stressed physicians who were decompressing from their intense lifestyle. After a short while they became warm and outgoing, and I grew close to and fond of them.

Sometimes we only begin to understand our passengers much later in the trip, or even afterwards, when some event explains an odd tick in their behavior, when some piece of information reveals what was happening beneath the surface. On one expedition, a woman in her thirties remained virtually mute and just plain strange for nearly five days, until—without prompting, and at the very moment I was rowing into a lively Class III rapid—she blurted out the story of how her boyfriend was paralyzed in a river accident several years before.

On another trip, I observed a frenetic type-A corporate attorney from New York sitting on a riverside boulder for two hours one evening, watching fish and shaking his head. He, too, was quiet for long stretches of our journey, but at the trip dinner at Jonathan's on the night of our take-out, he offered a toast and announced that this had been the most powerful experience of his life. I learned later that he divorced his wife as soon as he returned home.

I also remember an eighty-three-year old man who missed his airplane flight for a trip a few years ago and drove twenty-six hours by himself, without stopping, to reach the put-in for a Main Salmon trip just before we pushed off—as if he knew that he'd die of heart failure the following winter, and that this was, indeed, his final opportunity to float the river he loved.

Traveling with guests in the backcountry reminds us to look deeper, to be patient, and to seek explanations, rather than responding out of anger or frustration and missing the lessons our passengers can teach.

Even more than the distinct individuals who make up a trip, every group provides its own lessons about the human frontier. Although many of our guests share a common socio-economic status, they vary so greatly in age, religion, politics, background, and experience that you couldn't gather a more diverse and unpredictable collection of characters if you held a casting call for a production of *Paint Your Wagon*. Our challenge is to maximize everyone's experience by melding these distinct personalities into a cohesive, supportive, and mutually respectful group. Such a dynamic is essential when we ask them to form a line to haul gear up to camp, gather wood, or undertake some other group initiative.

In spite of our occasional peacemaking efforts, sometimes a couple of passengers simply decide to dislike each other. I nearly had to break up a fight one evening in camp after one guest unwittingly polished off a couple of cans of Diet Coke that another guest had brought along because it was all his kids would drink. On another trip, two World War II veterans—a Frenchman who'd been a German prisoner of war, and an American who'd fought against the Vichy French—got into a rather heated exchange regarding how they felt about each other's birth nations.

It's also revealing to watch how different folks in a group might respond to the same event, and how their reactions offer implicit keys to who they are. Lonnie told me a story about how one morning he convinced his group to wake up early and settle for a silent cold breakfast in the hopes that they might see some wildlife. After they witnessed a mountain lion killing a deer practically right in camp, one guest—an experienced Forest Service ranger—said it was the most remarkable thing he'd ever seen in the backcountry. A couple of kids on the trip weren't very impressed because they'd watched exactly this sort of thing on a National Geographic special. Another guest was annoyed that they hadn't gotten up this early every morning if that's when such events occurred.

Still, regardless of their different takes on situations and events, the river works to bond group members. Folks grow oddly close as soon as they've ridden together in a dory through the rollicking waves in Gunbarrel Rapid or over the big drop in Salmon Falls; or not long after they've soaked in Barth Hot Springs or shared a meal on a sun-warmed beach, or gathered around the fire, or undertaken a tough hike; or when they've been through something—nearly anything new and challenging—and expressed fear and excitement and harmonized their yells in the clean, misty air. Group members who weather a storm, or face some other adversity with dignity and by helping each other, will form the kinds of connections that even old friends may never develop.

Week after week we watch these amazing dynamics unfurl. Every trip offers its own lessons, its own unique personalities and occurrences. Kurt Wald says that he's learned an incredible amount about how to raise—and how not to raise—children. After a trip with particularly badly behaved kids, he rushes to the drugstore to buy more condoms. Sandra Gaskill likens trip dynamics to a group therapy session, and as she pursues a degree in sports psychology she'd like to bring families or other groups into the backcountry for intense counseling.

Both the best and worst passengers teach the group and the boatmen plenty and strongly influence the feeling of a trip. Though we have the responsibility of trying to help them be the best passengers they can be, and maximizing their experience, they determine what happens.

The best passengers know this already because it's the way they live their entire lives. This attitude may have inspired them to take a river trip in the first place. Such passengers possess a built-in capacity for wonder, a willingness to take risks, and a deeply-felt sense of adventure.

D.L. describes them this way: "The best passengers are inclined to be open-minded but they're also pretty romantic, whether or not they acknowledge that. They immediately recognize the romance in this kind of experience—not just in the trip, not just surrounding the boats or the river, but in the whole experience—and they are open to change and to looking at things in new ways. Artistic people—even people who don't think of themselves as artistic or creative—are especially touched. They see more and get a lot more out of a river trip. People who can entertain themselves and find interesting things wherever they are. People who'll explore the place and themselves. People who've gotten caught up in the workaday world but deep down still have this heroic nature that hasn't been allowed to come out. It reawakens when they're out on the river, but it takes some time."

My own best passengers possessed these qualities but they also tried to take responsibility for themselves. They wanted to be active participants in the expedition rather than just along for the ride—folks like John, a wiry high-tech computer guy from New Jersey who crushed all our tin and aluminum cans in camp every morning because he felt he should contribute in some way (and because he loved smashing things with a heavy stone); people like Mike from Chicago who commuted down to the boats each morning to help us load; folks who took the initiative to wander off and explore without being led on an organized hike. People who embraced the trip—and the territory—as their own.

My very worst passengers of the season were a group of thirty Boy Scouts, plus their three utterly uninvolved leaders who set up their own camp each evening as far from the boys as they could get. Although the scouts were individually fun and polite, as a troop they inflicted the highest impact on the environment of any group I've ever guided into the backcountry. Rather than taking responsibility and picking up after themselves, they left a trail of candy wrappers and personal belongings strewn through camp each morning and evening.

They also got so hyped on sugar every day that they would have been difficult to control even with the help of their worthless, apathetic leaders. We were annoyed enough by these leaders after just the first afternoon that Joel, who was the T.L., figured a way to get even with them.

Although the menu called for serving five boxes of cookies at lunch each day, Joel decided to ration the scouts to two or three boxes—especially since we'd caught them beginning their mornings by downing concoctions of hot cocoa mixed with honey and brown and white sugar. Joel stored the extra cookies in a rocket box in one of his dory hatches, and by the last day he'd collected fifteen boxes of Fig Newtons, Nutter Butters, and Oreos. Just when we hit the take-out, and right before the scouts were to climb aboard a school bus for a five-hour drive to Boise with only their leaders to watch over and control them, Joel announced that he had a small parting gift for these passengers from hell. He handed a half box of cookies to every scout to ensure that they'd be peaking on sugar just as their drive got underway.

With all that we do for good passengers—and most are good or even great—and all that they give us in return, a special bond develops. It's the most powerful and inspiring and also the most painful aspect of taking folks down the river. We share confidences during our time together—maybe partly because we know we'll never see each other again, but also because barriers break down out here and we want to reach out and make a connection. A woman who rode in my dory one afternoon described her pain at having decided to stay with a husband who didn't want children; another guest confessed that he'd left his wife recently and taken up with a much younger woman. A European guest named Roger, who reminded me of my grandfather, said one evening as we sipped Merlot before dinner that in spite of our slight language barrier, some people understood each other without having to speak.

These bonds between us and our passengers also form far more subtly, as when an older man was worried about his ability to go on a long hike, and I promised to keep an eye on him and hike at his pace and turn back any time he felt like it, as a way of encouraging him past his nervousness. Similarly, I confessed some of my own fears to certain special passengers—about my inadequacies as a guide, about troubling aspects of my intimate relationships. Spending time in the embrace of wilderness opened me up not just to other folks, but also to myself.

Upon finishing our week together in the backcountry, many passengers are reluctant to leave, afraid of breaking the connection to where they've been and what they've felt and even—for at least a time—who they've become. They might hover around the van that's to drive them away, reticent to board. At such moments they already know that as soon as they head for the airport to catch flights back to Los Angeles or Dallas or New York, once they step back inside their familiar lives, once they abdicate their place on the frontier, all the possibilities they believed in along the river may slowly begin to fade.

Boatmen somehow keep passengers' hopes alive—which is why some of them leave $1000 tips and write to us over the winter. Simply by being out here, by living this western dream, we sustain the myth that Americans have always needed: that a wilder, individualistic place still exists, and that such a life is still possible.

Some of these guests are unforgettable, and we know that we'll miss them for a long time to come. Saying good-bye hurts because even as we exchange addresses and promise to look each other up in Boston or Seattle or Denver, we know that the river is probably the only place our lives will ever converge. We come from different worlds, and though we've shared some incredible times together, we'll each go back to who we were: they'll be lawyers and doctors and parents again, folks who may look once in a while at the pictures of a special summer vacation and remember it fondly. And we'll head back down the river with another group that might be making their way to Lewiston or Boise even as we drive back from the take out. Ultimately, we must let go of our feelings for our passengers, because there's never any place to put them—just as we know that our love for the river will forever go unrequited.

Yet even our good-byes provide their discreet humor, irony, and subtleties. One beautiful summer evening, as our entire group walked out to the parking lot behind Jonathan's Restaurant after a trip dinner, Stew, who was our first commercial passenger ever to run the Middle Fork, Main, and Lower Salmon on a single trip, caught sight of Brannon's red 1963 Corvair parked beside our company van. This was the first car Stew ever drove, and he hadn't seen one in years. He began telling us stories about the adventures he'd had in that car, and in the middle of one tale, Brannon handed him the keys.

A few moments later, Stew drove off with his button-down shirt-sleeves rolled up and his elbow out the window, with Brannon riding beside him up front and Trista leaning forward from the back seat, the guest in control now, the guides his passengers.

On the Personal Frontier: Jeff 3, Jell-O Desserts 1

"The great appeal of the Turner thesis...comes from the fact that it depicts a universal problem that each person in his individual development attempts to solve."
Allan Beckman, *Hidden Themes in the Frontier Thesis: An Application of Psychoanalysis to Historiography*

"Take all the things you're bad at and fully concentrate on those for a year. Those are the things you need to embrace. You're going to enjoy the challenge of doing them better, with less pain, every time, until they are so easy that it doesn't even slow you down to think about them."
Brannon Riceci, River Guide

"The river provides a perfect environment—there are no distractions, no phones, people forget about time and focus on beauty and serenity and each other and on the river itself. All these factors take people's minds off their hectic, crazy lives at home. They allow people to enjoy and reflect and say, 'Wow, this is great fun,' or, 'This is challenging,' or, 'I hate this,' and also to ask, 'Why? What is it about me that's prompting this?'"
Sandra Gaskill, River Guide

My first assignment of the summer—when the river flowed high and muddy and roared between its banks—was to row a gear boat on a twelve-day Main/Lower Salmon trip. I hadn't rowed whitewater in two years, and I felt nervous about proving to the other guides that I could hold my own. I also needed to reassure myself that I knew what I was doing. It didn't help matters that right before the trip, Curt Chang pulled me aside for a "pep talk."

"You're going to have to prove a lot of people wrong this summer," Curt said, running a hand through his hair. "They seem to think of you as a celebrity boatman,"—meaning I was a guy who showed up for one or two trips each season, often with friends as paying passengers, and never really learned the systems or perfected my skills.

But in spite of the additional pressure from Curt, I ran all the whitewater pretty cleanly all that week, possibly because so many of the more technical rapids were washed out...until we came to Chittam Rapid on the last day of the Main section of the trip. From where we scouted the whitewater from a jumble of boulders on river right, the rapid looked HUGE. It was clear that you had to enter on the left side of a green tongue of smooth water at the top while pulling right to gain enough momentum to punch through a lateral wave (which came sideways off shore, perpendicular to the main current), thereby escaping the main current. By slipping into slower water you could avoid the humongous waves just left of center that piled into a sheer wall fifty yards downstream.

Not that it's much of an excuse, but just before we set out, one of the passengers who had been paddling an inflatable kayak decided Chittam was too intimidating. He wanted to ride in a dory, and so Sandra (who was training in my raft) and I strapped his inflatable kayak across our stern. It didn't occur to me to compensate for the extra drag or to consider that it might slow my momentum just a bit. But regardless of whether that had any effect or not, I blew my entry. I floated into the tongue above Chittam too far left, without enough rightward momentum, and didn't pull toward the lateral soon enough. Since I had angled my boat perpendicular to the current to row away from the big waves, the river carried me into them sideways. As the right side of my raft climbed up on the first big, murky wave to nearly ninety degrees vertical, I began to slide out the low side and into the water.

It happened very slowly, and I was amazed at how calm I remained, amazed to have the time to think about swimming through Chittam and avoiding getting pinned by the current against the wall below. But as I fell out of the boat, Sandra high-sided on the front tube, the raft dipped over the first wave and pitched up on the opposite side, and I slammed into the metal oarlock—all of which kept me in the craft.

At that same moment, my left oar shot out of the water, propelled by the power of the rapid, and cracked me in the head. Then, as the other side of the raft rose again, the river pinned the opposite oar blade underneath it. When at last the rapid spit us into calmer water, I scrambled back to my seat and pulled on the oars, but one didn't respond very well. It felt as if I kept missing the stroke. When I looked down, I saw that the oar had snapped in half and the blade was floating in the river nearby. I popped a spare oar into the stanchions and pulled the raft to shore before we approached Vinegar Rapid just around the corner.

The incident was unsettling and I cursed myself for performing so pathetically in a mere Class III rapid. I apologized profusely to Sandra and tried out a few excuses on her to explain my sorry run. I was as angry as I was shaken and ashamed. I couldn't summon an ounce of self-forgiveness or good humor, or manage to marvel at my luck at not going for a swim. It was as if I'd committed some atrocity—cheated the orphanage, or allowed the loyal family retriever to perish in a house fire. It was as if I'd proven myself worthy of every negative thing anyone had ever said of me. Running Chittam so badly wasn't something I'd done: it became who I was.

One of the most powerful and unpredictable aspects of crossing into the frontier is that at the moment you enter wild new territory you're often so focused on the challenge and the novelty—whatever form it takes—that you don't really see the nature of the new terrain. You perceive that it's unfamiliar, but you're not sure exactly how. You're more aware of the territory you've left than the place you've entered into.

After my horrific run in Chittam, I assumed that my own personal frontier consisted of the wild terrain of rowing whitewater, and that to succeed in this new land I needed to develop my skills until they were flawless. If I were a good enough rower, I figured, I'd never feel the inadequacy I experienced below Chittam; I'd be safe from criticism, and my self-image would remain secure.

It's clear to me now that the outward frontier often parallels something internal; in confronting any external challenge—whether by venturing into new places, taking up a sport like rock climbing, or going farther in a relationship than you ever have before—you necessarily encounter its inner, personal manifestation, as well.

It took a bad cheesecake to really bring this lesson home to me.

One evening on the Lower section of that same twelve-day trip, Brannon and I were cooking dinner together with the help of a massive Tanqueray and tonic. The air was hot and dry, and I sipped freely from the icy drink in spite of the fact that the kitchen was still unfamiliar territory. While Brannon attended to most of the chores that required skill, knowledge, confidence, or intuition, he assigned me easy tasks—probably to get me out of the way and reduce the risk of my screwing something up. I took it upon myself to make the salad and the instant Jell-O Brand cheesecake dessert, which comes in a box complete with step-by-step directions. All I had to do was add margarine to the crust, add milk to the filling, mess around a bit, slice a few kiwis on top, and stick the whole thing in the cool bottom of a dory hatch to chill.

But somehow in the course of drinking a lot of gin, searching for extra milk and not finding any, and realizing I'd have to pump a few cups of drinkable water and use it to mix up some powdered milk, I added the water to the cake filling without ever actually adding the powdered milk to the water. So just before dessert, when I went to retrieve my cheesecake from the dory, it looked like a bubbly swamp with bright green kiwi fruit sinking in the muck. I tried peeling off the kiwi and adding the dried milk right then to thicken it up, but I was too late. With no other dessert to offer a group of hungry passengers, I finally just set out the mixture and called it cheesecake mousse pie.

The nice thing about cooking on the river is that most guests are extremely appreciative of whatever you do. As Brannon likes to say, "You could serve them gruel and they'd lap it up like dogs." Which they did. But the other guides and I still knew that with this cheesecake incident I'd somehow managed to screw up the dessert equivalent of making toast.

So rather than adopting an attitude of non-attachment and taking the whole silly event in stride, I allowed this ruined cheesecake to add to the burden of and assume the same weight and psychic feel as nearly flipping my boat in Chittam and nearly having a bad swim a few days earlier. On the surface I made as if to laugh it off. But it grew heavy inside me.

And I didn't just let it go there. Throughout the course of the summer, each time I spotted an instant Jell-O dessert on the menu, I made a point of confessing my story and volunteering to take on the cheesecake or chocolate mousse pie as if I had something important to prove. I'm happy to report that by the end of my season, the final score stood at Jeff 3, Jell-O desserts 1. Which entirely misses the point.

Until I came to Idaho to work as a river guide for the entire season, it never occurred to me that I might have chosen my career as a writer at least partly as a way of never having to work with other people.

The summer proved difficult for me in a couple of ways. First of all, I suddenly found myself—a solitary writer—working with and around twenty or thirty people every day. Which would have been hard enough in itself because, like many folks, I worry a little too much about what other people might be thinking of me; but it was that much tougher because the work all these people saw me doing involved many things I couldn't do well, at least early in the season.

So, if I broke an oar or ruined the cheesecake at dinner—funny and inconsequential events—and everyone laughed and gave me good-natured grief, I missed the humor in it because I felt as if they were laughing at who I was, not at something goofy that I'd done. It felt as if my very identity was caught up in the cheesecake, and I was being judged on it.

I have seen other guides demonstrate grace and poise after

screwing up in both minor and major ways: Leon after cracking his dory into a wall in flat water in Green Canyon; Chris Quinn after forgetting half our trip gear; Brannon after cooking cloves too long in the brandied pears one night so that our tongues went numb and fat and we couldn't understand each other's speech; Robert Henry after setting up the table incorrectly one morning, so that the entire coffee and tea service crashed into the sand at Rhett Creek Camp; and countless other guides performing stupid, careless, funny human *faux pas*.

I didn't recognize the Zen purity of maintaining your balance in such circumstances until after my last trip was over and there were no more meals to cook or rapids to run or passengers to get to know, when there were no more opportunities for letting go of pride and control. I didn't understand that my own challenge was to focus not on events themselves, but on my response to them, because that provides a far better measure of who we really are.

The frontier, I came to see, has this ability to work things below the surface, to present challenges we may not even be aware of until they've already changed us. It's not until the mountain man returns to civilization that he realizes he's no longer of the place that was once his home; or, to put it more profoundly, sometimes Jell-O cheesecakes are more than just desserts.

Camp

> *"...our kind has lived in wilderness at least one hundred times longer than it has lived in civilization. Certainly the influence of this immense background of collective experience would not disappear easily or completely...*
>
> *"...Alexis de Tocqueville resolved to see wilderness during his 1831 trip to the United States, and in Michigan Territory in July the young Frenchman found himself at last on the fringe of civilization. But when he informed the frontiersmen of his desire to travel for* pleasure *into the primitive forest, they thought him mad."*
>
> RODERICK NASH, *WILDERNESS AND THE AMERICAN MIND*

The moment that we slide the boats up onto the sand at Cow Palace Camp on the Lower Gorge in the mid-afternoon, a young couple from San Diego leaps into shallow water and hits the beach like MacArthur in the Philippines. They charge the hill and throw down a couple of sweatshirts and a small dry bag and two baseball caps on a wide, flat spot at the top of the rise as if planting their nation's flag upon some newly conquered territory.

On this same day, an older guest traveling by himself helps us unload all the boats and then waits patiently by the river as we decide where to set up the unit. Once he learns its location, he lugs his dry bag to the opposite end of camp and unrolls his sleeping tarp to stake out his own little homestead far from the world. He neatly arranges his ammo can, hiking boots, water bottle, and flashlight in predetermined positions around the edges of the tarp, and lays his dry bag at the head of his sleeping bag as a sort of back-rest or pillow. Finally, he places a framed picture of his wife in the sand to complete the illusion of a cozy bedroom.

Camp: the very word imparts the cushy feel of an inflated air mattress. It confirms that the day's wanderings and travails have ended. It promises comfort, quiet, a hot meal, a cold drink, a soft, warm place to pull around you when the night grows chilly and dark. Regardless of the style or strategy involved, the mere act of placing a few personal items on the ground, or spreading out a sleeping bag, or pitching a tent, allows you to feel as if you've claimed a place for yourself out here in the backcountry, transforming it into a private retreat you can think of—at least for the night—as "home." It's an illusion, of course—because bad weather or a rattlesnake or a twisted ankle could quickly remind you of how far from the world you really are—but an illusion we embrace.

There is something about setting up your own private camp spot that proclaims to the ambivalent wilderness, "I am here now. I matter! This is my turf." One guest this summer—a Milwaukee detective—was so territorial about defining his personal space that he jokingly strung up yellow tape around his sleeping bag that read "POLICE LINE: DO NOT CROSS." But such assertiveness simultaneously whispers, "Please, oh, please protect me from predators, bad weather, crazy mountain men, and various other potential forms of discomfort, unpleasantness, and acts of God."

A lot of people don't feel as if camp is really home until they pitch their tents. Although guides actively encourage guests not to sleep indoors on a river trip—and most folks spend at least a night or two under the stars—many people take comfort in knowing their tent is set up nearby in much the same way that little kids camping in the yard are gladdened by a light in the kitchen. Whether this tent thing satisfies some primal urge for shelter or simply allays a fear of late-night storms I can't say; but I do know that in a steady downpour there's nothing more reassuring than stowing your gear safely inside a sturdy, spacious nylon dome, climbing in, and lying back in dry comfort as drops patter a staccato rhythm on the rain fly outside.

While our passengers devise the personal floor plans of their bedrooms and mess with tent poles, we guides set up the bathroom, give shape to the kitchen, and maybe even hang a couple of solar showers from a tree or arrange the inflatable kayaks on their sides in the sand like couches around the fire pan. In a half hour we will have temporarily renovated and redefined the beach, lending it familiar if rough amenities. By evening, we may sip Chardonnay and munch hors d'oeuvres and mingle as if attending a cocktail party at some bigshot's gorgeous country estate, with the river playing like soft music in the background and the view as pastel and inviting as a landscape painting—if somewhat less predictable. We will have taken the first steps toward converting the backcountry into something more manageable. But the beauty of river travel is that by morning, when we break down camp, pack up, and float away, we'll have erased all evidence of our stay. We'll restore the site to its pristine condition, and by that evening, we'll encounter an entirely new and different locale. The comfort will have been mostly in our perception; we will have left the wilderness still wild.

Each night of a river trip we hunker down in camps named for natural features: Deep Hole, Twin Snags, Rattlesnake Bar, Yellow Pine Bar; or named after early settlers: Lantz Bar, Wilson Bar,

Hermit Hank's, Blackadar, Myers Creek; or named to imply a story about the site: Gold Rush Bar, Hungry Bar, Sunny Bar, Engine Block, Cow Palace, Wickiup Bar, Poor Bar; or named after tributary streams: Bargamin Creek, California Creek, Disappointment Creek.

If the river is a tongue, camps are the words it forms. Each camp expresses its own very distinct personality and feel. Some are wide and exposed to the elements—great on a calm, clear night for viewing the Perseids meteor shower in August, but not the place to get caught in a wind storm. Others offer the protection of stately pines, the ground beneath them blanketed with soft, dry needles, boughs shaking above in breezy percussion. Some are small and narrow, framed by rocky slopes or steep cliffs, and make for a tighter community feel.

Different camps may determine a group's experiences and even their emotional states while they're there. A deep eddy off shore soothes and relaxes and invites contemplation; camps close to fast-moving water seem more frenetic. A long, lazy view downriver eases people's minds about what's ahead tomorrow. Open slopes behind camp, and expansive views of high ridges seem to draw folks out of themselves. Sometimes we're forced to settle for a scrubby, makeshift camp if our intended destination is occupied. This can prove disappointing—even depressing—and cause rampant crankiness, or draw a group closer together, the way being stranded together in a snowstorm or a blackout might.

Since many of our guests have never slept outside before, and many others have never passed a night along a wild river, our first camp may set precedents and even shape their perceptions and realities. They take cues, assuming that however we do things on that initial evening is how things are necessarily done. If it's raining, and we all pitch tents, this group will pitch their tents every night, even if the sky is water-clear after day two. If we play a game around the fire to help folks get to know each other, they'll gather in a circle every night, expecting some sort of organized activity.

Although I'm against dragging along even more gear than we already carry, chairs are the one item that can really affect group dynamics in camp. By setting chairs up in a circle just before dinner, we create a communal space where group members will come together and face each other; otherwise, guests may cluster in small family groups, eating separately because they're uncertain as to how they're supposed to behave.

The best camps combine a number of different features in the same way that a well-designed estate home blends architectural elements. A good place to park dories is an essential requirement—a sandy landing area out of the current and far enough from jet boat-induced surges to keep the boats from moving much. It's always nice to camp near a whispering riffle, but not too close to a major rapid, which may exclaim so loudly that passengers will have to shout at one another to be heard. Lower Richardson Bar camp sits just above Big Mallard Rapid, and so while you're trying to relax on the beach, the river draws your eye toward the whitewater and you marvel at tomorrow's run, and how narrow the slot between a giant pourover and the left shore appears. A big eddy is also a nice camp feature, for fishing, swimming, and water games.

The very best camps offer shade in the heat of the day but also gather good light late into the evening and catch early sun in the morning to help ease you out of your sleeping bag in the cool hours. They encompass flat ground for sleeping, ball-playing, and setting up the kitchen. A side creek provides a good place for exploring or sitting beside after dinner as you contemplate the wonders of your life. A nearby homestead is also great; Rhett Creek camp sits just downstream of the old Wolfe place, and on some trips we're lucky enough to see the family matriarch hanging out laundry or working in the yard. Yellow Pine Bar camp is just a short walk from where a British couple caretakes a beautiful spread on a thirty-six-acre parcel of private land, and occasionally we'll wander up there and marvel at the apples and plums and snap peas hanging heavy in the garden, or sit on the porch stairs and listen to their stories.

But what seems like the perfect camp at one water level may transform into an entirely different place at another. On one early-season trip, when the water was high, we passed an idyllic evening under the pines at Corey Bar. Later in the season, at low water, it took us several hours longer to get there because of the slower current. And whereas in June we'd floated right into the heart of camp and unloaded easily, in August we had to maneuver the boats through a shallow channel and park in deep black mud, which made carrying gear a slightly dangerous yet highly comical affair.

Choosing the right camp for a particular group on a specific night—do they need space to spread out, or should we push them close to help them bond; do we want a beach for volleyball and horseshoes, or a place to hike—is one of the Trip Leader's many challenges, especially since there are no guaranteed camps. Because the Forest Service and Bureau of Land Management (BLM) don't preassign camps on the Main or Lower, you never know for sure where you might end up on a given night as the light fades in the afternoon and you scramble to find a good and unoccupied spot.

Outfitters often vie for the same popular sites, so to avoid competition, occasionally we negotiate camps at the put-in, trading our preferred choice for the first night for a prime spot on the second night. Some beer may change hands, and negotiations may turn raucous—festive, even. On the water, whenever we row past other groups, or they float past us, we confer with their leaders to see where they're planning to camp.

All is pretty friendly on the Main, but since good camps are scarce on the Lower Salmon, some companies have taken to sending runners downstream in the morning, ahead of their groups, to claim a camp that their other boats might not arrive at for another five hours. Which is not only illegal, it's bad etiquette—not the kind of behavior that would lead another outfitter to stop and help you unwrap a boat from a rock in Snow Hole Rapid, for example, if you got stuck there one day during a summer you'd been stealing camps.

For my money, I love to camp in a spot I've never been to before because it increases the potential for discovery—new streams to hike up, new ridges to explore, and a better chance to come across something memorable. During the trip on which I rowed the Morro Rock for twelve days, our group was small enough to take the unusual camp at Sheep Creek, which turned out to be one of my favorites along the entire Main Salmon. We slid the dories into a sandy cove like books onto a shelf, and tucked the kitchen between boulders just a few yards from shore. I set up my own private sleeping spot on a raised, flat beach close enough to the river to hear fish jumping and splashing, and the gentle whir of the current. The rest of the group chose spots of flat sand separated by boulders that made each feel like a private bedroom. Behind camp, a trail wound upstream along Sheep Creek, and I hiked there before dinner, communing with the cold, clear water and picking wild raspberries that made the perfect topping for the chocolate mousse pie (bringing the score to Jeff 2, Jell-O desserts 1). One guest claimed to have caught nearly thirty trout in a couple of hours of joyous fly fishing in the creek. And in the morning, as we were breaking camp, a herd of big horn sheep wandered into the kitchen trying to get close to a mineral lick on a rock.

On rare occasions—particularly early in the season when the water is high and fast and it's easy to make a lot of miles quickly, or on longer trips—we may take the extreme luxury of a layover day and camp in the same place for two nights. On layovers, camp really begins to feel like home. You form attachments to a particular view of creek water cascading past green ferns, or the way a smooth rock seems to welcome a prone body lying in the sun. There's nothing quite like wilderness leisure—drinking your coffee on the edge of camp where water meets sand without having to think about an imminent departure; heading out on a hike (or not) whenever you feel like it, and returning later to a familiar place where all your gear is organized and laid out for immediate use, and snacks are handy in the kitchen, and a cooler of icy drinks sits in the shade beneath a big old Ponderosa pine, and a good book awaits you.

But just as everyone must leave home eventually, there comes that time when we have to break camp and move on. Even if the day promises great rapids and new adventures, there's something sad about departing from a pretty spot just as it begins to grow comfortable. I always feel a sort of longing, too: much like driving through a neighborhood and wishing I could spend some time getting to know the nuances of each house, the comfort of a certain chair pulled up in front of a south-facing window, the clatter of dishes heard from a porch off the kitchen. I wish for the chance to walk slowly, humming, up a slope behind camp just to see the river curl around a bend downstream, or swim in a sun-drenched eddy, or lean back against a log in the sand and read in the shade, or simply watch golden light slide down the face of a cliff across the water as the day fades toward dusk. I want to know every mood of this territory, but I recognize that would comprise a lifetime's work.

Over the entire course of the summer, I always craved just a little more time in each camp, one more degree of intimacy. But the river flows, and we must inevitably put back out on it and give ourselves over to the current again, moving downstream to that next camp, that next unknown site that we'll barely come to know before we push on once more.

Side Trips

"Even though I've been down the river many times, when you see it in different weather or different light it's always got these little treasures, like an Easter egg hunt. It's very familiar, yet there's always something unexpected around the corner."
DON LITTON (D.L.), RIVER GUIDE

"Always it has been the frontier which has allured many of our boldest souls. And always back of the frontier, advancing, receding, crossing it this way and that, succeeding and failing, hoping and despairing, but steadily advancing in the net result has come that portion of the population which builds homes and lives in them..."
EMERSON HOUGH, *THE PASSING OF THE FRONTIER*

It's late morning on day four of the Boy Scout trip, and as we float around a bend in the river, past the ruins of the old Painter Mine, we catch our first glimpse of the wide, sandy beach at Five Mile Bar.

"Is this it? Is this Buckhorn Bill's?" one of the boys asks. His friends, who've been inquiring about this stop every ten minutes since yesterday morning, look on expectantly.

"Buck*skin* Bill's," I say.

"Is this it?" they all ask at once.

Up ahead of us, Joel has already begun rowing the Lake Tahoe toward the beach, thus answering their questions. He was the one who tried to excite the troop yesterday with the prospect of visiting an old homestead where the last of the mountain men lived until only fifteen years ago. Joel also mentioned the possibility (I don't know what he was thinking) of ice cream.

As we drift through the eddy toward the Bar, a volleyball net and three pink plastic flamingos welcome us from the sand. Beyond the crescent beach we can just make out a few buildings tucked back in the trees. To our left stands the stone gun turret tower that Buckskin built when the U.S. government tried to evict him from his land back in the seventies. Apparently Buckskin told the Feds that if they wanted him to leave they'd have to shoot him out. The government eventually deferred.

I tie up my boat and follow the boys up the steps to the compound—past the sign welcoming us to the Buckskin Bill Museum, past the room full of rifles, pistols, powder horns, tools, brass cookware, elk hide rugs, and deerskin clothing, all of which Buckskin designed and manufactured out here in the wilderness; past the antlers and arrowheads and animal skulls, hunting trophies and other artifacts; beyond the adobe structure that Buckskin used as a bedroom; just short of the massive garden ripening in the sun; and in through the second door on the left, where Barbara—one of two resident caretakers (the other is her husband, Heinz)—is handing ice cream sandwiches over the counter in exchange for pairs of dollar bills. In a moment of cynicism, it strikes me that these days, Buckskin Bill comes in a distant second to the dollar bill as the preferred currency of Five Mile Bar.

Even when the scouts finish clamoring to buy candy and ice cream (the troop, from Beverly Hills, drops $300 on sweets in the half hour we're here), the boys fail to notice they're in a museum that celebrates everything pure and good and exciting about the West, about self-sufficiency and rugged individualism. It doesn't occur to them—or they just don't care—that everything around them here is real; this isn't Frontierland at the Magic Kingdom. As their first sugar high of the day starts kicking in, they run back down to the beach to wrestle and water fight and throw sand at each other, while up in the museum a video about Buckskin Bill plays to an empty room.

If they'd watched the video, or picked up one of the books, or looked at some of the displays, they'd have learned that Sylvan Hart—who acquired the name "Buckskin Bill" because of his preferred wardrobe—came to the Salmon River during the Great Depression and lived here until his death in 1980. During that time—in addition to fashioning his own clothes—Buckskin raised an extensive garden, hunted game, prospected, studied subjects ranging from Geology to Greek, cooked and baked from scratch, entertained visitors, explored the region, and made his own knives, rifles, cookware, and just about anything else he ever needed. According to Buckskin himself, he usually spent about $50 a year on supplies. He also spent as much time as he could with surviving Salmon River old-timers to learn their stories and pick up a few tips on preparing bear or placering for gold. Harold Peterson has written a fine book about Buckskin, entitled *The Last of the Mountain Men,* that describes his life in colorful detail.

Buckskin provided a sort of segue along the Salmon River—between the real frontier and the present, when the frontier is mostly mythical. He epitomized everything the rugged American individualist should be, even at a time when living that way was barely possible anymore. In spite of his eventual popularity with commercial river passengers, Buckskin's life of solitude and self-sufficiency more closely resembled how the first pioneers lived than we're ever likely to see again. Folks who take the time to consider his legacy are often moved and inspired.

Today Heinz and Barbara caretake Five Mile Bar, which they've converted into this museum that both celebrates Buckskin and the frontier, and simultaneously parodies them by offering beer, film, ice cream, and tee-shirts for sale. Nobody can blame the couple for trying to make a living, and Heinz is deeply committed to preserving the spirit of backcountry life along the river, but it's still ironic that they've transformed the last outpost of the last true mountain man into a float-through Quik Mart. What's more ironic is that many folks who visit the Salmon River to experience wildness are more interested in buying a Snickers Bar than in recognizing or appreciating this last remnant of the frontier as more than a candy store.

In terms of neat places to stop at along the river, places that provide a sense of carving a life out of the wilderness, I much prefer visiting Newt and Sharon, who have caretaken a couple of cabins on Yellow Pine Bar—with seventeen cats and one dog—for nearly two decades. Pioneers have occupied the bar since the late 1800s, and it once boasted a one-room schoolhouse. Today, Newt and Sharon live in a house that earlier residents erected in 1948, and to which they've added a second floor. Floating the river past the bar, we can glimpse their porch and lattice work covered with flowers, their local telephone line (battery operated), and the wind sock beside their landing strip.

Walking up to the thirty-six-acre spread with a group of passengers, we usually encounter Newt and his dog working in the garden. The dog is always frantically excited by the prospect of visitors who might toss a Frisbee for him to chase. Newt is cordial and soft-spoken, taking the time from his chores to show us around, identifying the dozens of varieties of fruits and vegetables and even where he picked up the seed stock (he claims to have collected every edible species grown along the river), showing off his irrigation system and micro-hydro generating plant, and describing the history of the Bar. Inside the main house, he might open a jar of pickled garlic and pass it around for everyone to taste.

The couple of times I visited Yellow Pine, Newt's wife Sharon was upstairs watching auto racing on the satellite TV (powered by generator). Although they live hundreds of miles from the nearest place to drive a car fast, Newt and Sharon are fanatical auto racing fans. They receive several racing newspapers, and on certain Sundays they can watch races from all over the world starting at about five A.M. I discovered a beat-up old jeep parked behind their wood shed that they'd outfitted with a shiny Jaguar hood ornament.

In spite of the modern conveniences they've installed, and the jet boat occasionally parked out below the house, Newt and Sharon's place seems far more rustic to me than Five Mile Bar, perhaps because they make no pretense of running a museum, or even inviting folks to stop and visit. It's easier to imagine them living as Buckskin Bill did than it is to think of Heinz and Barbara really roughing it in Bill's old digs.

Occasionally we also look in on two other currently-occupied homestead sites along the river: the Polly Bemis Ranch and Rheo Wolfe's cabin. Charlie and Polly Bemis lived on the Bemis place before the turn of the century. The story goes that back in China, Polly's father sold her as an indentured servant to a Chinese miner, who later lost her to Bemis in a poker game. When a sore loser shot Bemis after another game, Polly nursed him back to health and the two eventually married. Today, managers of timeshare condos on the property offer guided tours of an old cabin, but you need a vivid imagination to feel the pulse of what this place was like before developers commercialized the site.

Rheo Wolfe's cabin isn't really open to visitors; we spy it from the river, or across a field of wildflowers when we camp at Rhett Creek. Mrs. Wolfe first came to the Salmon River in 1958; Carrey and Conley's book includes a picture of her standing in this same field teaching seven of her children to play the violin. The local school board once tried to charge her with contributing to the delinquency of minors after she began teaching her children at home, but nobody in town was willing to pursue the case. And the Forest Service challenged the family's mining claim, but Mrs. Wolfe walked twenty-seven miles to the hearing to prove they had a right to stay. Mrs. Wolfe and other family members spend part of their summers living in the old house.

The majority of Salmon River residents abandoned their cabins and other historic sites when—or in many cases long before—the Forest Service cleared folks out and burned many buildings after the Salmon was officially designated as a wilderness area in the seventies. But throughout the river corridor, a few surviving structures make for great hiking destinations.

Most commercial river trips stop in at Jim Moore's place, a favorite along the Main Salmon. Current occupants consist of the occasional bear, deer, elk, and coyotes who come to eat the fruit in Jim's old orchard. Moore, who lived here around the turn of the century, erected nine cabins in a huge clearing because he'd filed for the spot as a mining claim and had to build structures with the trees he felled. The Forest Service accidentally preserved Moore's buildings, and they were later nominated to the National Register of Historic Places.

Moore sold supplies to miners traveling along the Three Blaze Trail to the Thunder Mountain gold fields. He claimed that 1800 men passed through during the first two years of this century. He was also known to distill a few spirits—and not the kind that would spook you at night. You can visit Moore's grave and wooden headstone—which reads "Born about 1868, Died about April 25, 1942"—out behind the buildings. Since nobody occupies the site anymore, and there's nothing to buy, standing in Moore's wide clearing and looking at the ridges across the river, or at apples hanging heavy on the trees, you understand how lucky a man would have been to have lived here a hundred years ago.

In addition to these and other homestead sites, we also try to take passengers to at least one natural hot spring along the river. We usually stop to soak in Barth Hot Springs on the second morning of Main Salmon trips. Tucked into a slope a hundred feet above the river, Barth proves most welcoming on chilly, overcast days, when steam rises from the surface of the stone-and-cement soaking pool and clouds float through the valley below. A few years ago a porcelain bath tub still perched in a more isolated spot, but somebody's since removed it. Climbing into the hot water with our guests always feels like a special occasion; on my first trip here, we crowded in twelve college students wearing party hats to celebrate someone's birthday.

We also occasionally visit another, more remote hot springs farther down river. If we spend the night at French Creek or Robbins Creek, we'll hike the couple of miles up to the springs from camp. From French Creek, this involves either ferrying guests across the river in a dory, or riding across in an old wooden box suspended from a cable thirty feet above the river. Once across, we hike through the ruins of an old town that included a post office, school, and CCC camp.

You can access the hot springs themselves in two places: in a tiny, ramshackle bathhouse containing a mossy wooden tub, and in a dark cave that's filled with bats during the day. On one trip, we coaxed a group of guests into the bat cave, and once we were sitting in the warm water, turned off our flashlights. A passenger who'd proven himself to be particularly macho all week suddenly began bawling, and begged us to put the lights back on; apparently we'd discovered the parameters of his particular personal frontier. Loping back down the trail to camp after another visit, we collected a hat-full of fresh apricots right off a tree, and whipped them up into a tasty syrup for our pancakes the next morning.

In addition to these popular side trips, we also offer some kind of hike nearly every afternoon from camp—sometimes to a particular destination like a ridge-top or cabin or up along a side stream, and sometimes just for the sake of walking, because folks have been sitting in the boats all day and crave a little more activity. It often takes getting off the river and up into the surrounding country where people lived and hunted and passed by on their way to the mines, or to visit friends, for us really to get in touch with the character of this place. Every site spins stories of lovely, difficult days lived out here; every collapsed cabin, abandoned mine shaft, and old corral whispers a tale about the people who passed briefly over this land. Standing in their doorways or orchards, or walking along the paths they wore into the terrain over many years, we can feel something of their lives—and by so doing, feel something of our own.

Wild Adventure vs. Corporate Venture: The Business of Running Rivers

"Henry David Thoreau was your classical dilettante. O' course there never was a fellow who could write near so well about his creek going up or down an inch or two but Thoreau never did work at his job long enough to know what he was doing...

"A guy like...Thoreau never did come to grips with reality. He led too sheltered a life. If he had had a cabin surrounded by grizzlies and mountain lions and rabid coyotes and dance hall girls, that would have made a man of him. Westerners have had to survive all that."
BUCKSKIN BILL

"From a customer standpoint, if you're signing up for a trip and an outfitter says, 'We're not going to do anything for you, we're going to make you work,' you'd say, 'You've got to be nuts; I'm going to sign up for this trip over here where they put up my tent for me.'

"But it's still a frontier for passengers. What would it be like to sign up for this having never done anything like it before, never floated a river, or been in a raft, or set up a tent? Everything would

be new and mind-blowing. The only thing missing is that they don't have to be a part of the trip."
DON LITTON (D.L.), RIVER GUIDE

In the late afternoon at Groundhog Bar, the ridges above camp lie in deep, cool shadow, the lower beach stands in warm sun, and the waves in Whiplash Rapid rippling past just off shore sparkle in the golden, fading light. We've arrived here early enough to hike up to the old homestead at Jim Moore's Place. Upon returning, we fish and play horseshoes and relax as evening slides toward us along the horizon. I'm enjoying a perfectly fine mood until I spot one of my favorite passengers on this trip punching the buttons on something that looks an awful lot like a cellular phone.

At first glance I figure it's a joke. I know, for instance, that Leon carries a hollow plastic telephone-shaped flask in his dory that you can fill with liquids such as tequila and sip through the antenna. So I figure that's what Mike is doing: yukking it up for his family.

But I'm wrong. Here we are—camped on an idyllic beach on a warm afternoon in the middle of the River of No Return Wilderness, three days in, supposedly having left all the extraneous noise of society behind us—and Mike is calling his office. I'm extremely pleased when he can't get any reception, but he tells me he's been checking in every night and this is the first time the call hasn't gone through.

In an essay entitled *Walking*, Henry David Thoreau wrote, "Eastward I go only by force; but westward I go free... I must walk toward Oregon, and not toward Europe... Every sunset which I witness inspires me with the desire to go to a West as distant and fair as that into which the sun goes down... We dream all night of those mountain ridges in the horizon, though they may be of vapor only... The West of which I speak is but another name for the Wild; and what I have been preparing to say is that in Wildness is the preservation of the World."

Unlike Frederick Jackson Turner, Thoreau didn't identify an expanse of untrammeled land, or *wilderness* as the crucial western resource; rather, Thoreau celebrated *wildness*—a distinction which has great implications for the mythology of the American West, as well as for travelers on the Salmon River.

Wilderness is a place which hasn't been disturbed by human meddling, the natural configuration of the land in its original state: what lies just beyond the frontier. Wilderness—or what's left of it in America—is necessarily wild in and of itself, and provides a perfectly nice place to spend your time. The Salmon River canyon, with a few exceptions, is a wilderness.

The Salmon is also wild, but *wildness* is a quality that can be exhibited both by nature, and—intentionally—by man. And it is wildness, including the intentional act of being wild, that Thoreau advocates. Although spending time in the wilderness is a great start, that's not enough. We need to open ourselves up to wildness, and to act wildly, too. Wildness can transform any place or situation into a frontier.

Depending on your guides and fellow passengers, and your own behavior, a river trip on the Salmon can most certainly be wild. You could swim through rapids in your life jacket, dance naked around the fire at night playing sticks for percussion, or run barking into the darkness just to see what kind of critters you might scare up. For some folks, just setting up their own tent or sleeping outside might be pretty wild, while others will need to push themselves more, perhaps discovering wildness by paddling an inflatable kayak through Big Mallard Rapid. Wildness is a personal frontier. To experience it on a river trip, you might eschew every possible superfluous item dragged in from the real world (such as cellular telephones); to embrace it, you might face head on—with initiative and a welcoming smile—the multitude of challenges that confront you out in the backcountry.

I would agree with Thoreau that wildness is essential to our survival and growth. I would also agree with other writers, such as Turner, Ed Abbey, Wallace Stegner, Annie Dillard, and Barry Lopez, who suggest that wilderness—just one aspect of wildness—is equally important. And I would add that a week-long trip on the Salmon River, in the heart of the West, provides the perfect opportunity both to encounter wilderness and to act wild within it—but that these days it may require some real effort. Though many passengers still have transforming experiences on our trips, those experiences are becoming rarer and less intense as our trips become less wild.

Back when Martin Litton first started running dories in the Grand Canyon, and then up in Idaho, river trips were characterized by a genuine spirit of adventure. In those early, exploratory days, outfitters brought along minimal gear and prepared simple meals and offered passengers on each trip a uniquely unpredictable experience. Some nights, when the dinner dishes were air-drying in the warm dusk, guides might take a few guests out on their dories to go eddy cruising—drifting in wide, lazy circles for an hour or two just to feel the breath of the night while waiting for the moon to rise. Or they'd repack all their gear and put back out on the river in darkness, pulling into some camp at midnight just for the giddy pleasure of floating when the water was most beautiful. They spent afternoons exploring side canyons or hiking to the rim for the simple reason that none of them had ever been up there before. Nobody asked about their destination, or how long it would take; people understood that the journey itself was as important as getting anywhere; not knowing was the whole point.

In those days, a guide who went a whole trip without flipping his boat was having a great run. The early trips were characterized by great uncertainty. Even more surprising, passengers were considered integral, contributing members of those expeditions.

Don Litton, who took his first river trip with his father when he was twelve—and says he might have gone sooner if not for the home-movies of boats flipping and monster rapids that Martin was always showing—talks about those times with great longing. "In the early days we used to carry boats around certain rapids in the Grand Canyon, and everyone had to pitch in. They thought, 'I'm a part of this. I'm an agent in my own success. I'm not being taken down; I have to help. If I don't help, we may not make it.' I think it added to their trip when we said, 'Hey everybody, help us lift this boat.' And everybody—little old ladies, big strong men—even if they weren't lifting anything, even if they only had their finger on the boat, they were a part of making the trip go."

The early trips were especially magical because of the kinds of things that happened to those people who set themselves freely and open-mindedly in the wilderness as part of the expedition. To put it simply, they changed—sometimes right there on the river on day five or six, and other times after the trips. Every guide can tell stories about folks who returned home following a great river journey and quit their jobs, divorced their spouses, got married, moved to a new city, or otherwise envisioned their lives in new ways. Some even became river guides.

A week—or preferably more—participating in a trip along a pristine river gave people a chance to rise out of themselves in a way that may not have happened to them in years, if ever. Guests were often shocked to discover deep capacities for feelings they hadn't experienced since childhood. Free of the distractions and cultural anesthesia of society, in the quiet canyons, their real selves often made rare and unexpected appearances, coming to them like ghosts while they hiked along a stream or watched the river flowing past camp in an endless ribbon of green. People softened as each day drew them further from the world. They bonded with other passengers after being sullen and withdrawn. Someone would quit smoking; an eighty-year old woman hooted with delight as she tossed a bucket of river water on her equally elderly husband. Folks got so jacked on adrenaline going through a big rapid that they performed heroic high-sides to keep their dories from flipping.

D.L. told me about a friend of his whom he'd finally convinced to go on a Grand Canyon trip some years ago. "If I'd told her prior to the trip that she'd rappel down into a canyon knee-deep in a rushing stream, she would have said, 'That's not for me,' and she wouldn't have gone. Once she did it, she said that it changed her whole outlook on herself, her whole life. She said, once she saw she could do that, she felt she could do anything. People just feel a sense of elation—like when you first go rock climbing and you think you're going to die the whole way up and then you make it to the top and get this adrenaline rush and can't believe it."

Today, although our trips still exert powerful impacts on some passengers, it's the rare journey that doesn't come off with tame predictability. It's the exception when a boat wrecks or somebody swims through a bad rapid, or we hike folks up to some unique, hard-to-reach place. And it's more unusual for a passenger to experience some sort of epiphany. In these particularly litigious days, instead of asking guests to lift boats and help in the kitchen and even just take responsibility for themselves, we ask what we can do for them, would they like whole milk or two-percent in their coffee, can we fix them another Martini? We encourage dilettantism. We treat guests like visitors to a safari park, and only promote the illusion of adventure. We provide passengers with an opportunity to encounter the mythological West, but simultaneously shield them from confronting the unpredictable frontier substance that still remains.

One of my biggest regrets from this summer is that I agreed to help a young, fit, wealthy couple from California set up their tent every night. Steve, the husband, told me he was a good tipper, and that he'd make it worth my while (for the record: $20 is not a lot of money, even to a river guide). I succumbed mostly because at that early point in the season, I thought a good guide responded to a passenger's every expressed need. It wasn't until later that I figured out I'd really have been doing Steve a favor if I'd encouraged him to put up the tent himself.

Not only don't we require folks to participate and take ownership of their trips in any way; we've also begun providing extremes of service. We encourage passivity rather than responsibility and promise to take care of every possible whim that our passengers might have. Rather than organizing a hike that might maximize their wilderness experience or lead to some unexpected bit of spontaneity or discovery, we don aprons and spend most of our off-river time preparing ridiculously complex meals. Rather than giving a talk about the Nez Perce Indians, or exploring an abandoned mine site, or leading an interactive game that might bring the group closer together, we chop and peel vegetables, we wash romaine lettuce one leaf at a time, we triple-foil wrap a pork tenderloin and tend to it with obsessive care. A couple of guides have described the experience of river trips these days as "basically going out to eat in the wilderness."

Many of our passengers also drag as much dross as they can from the real world into the wilderness. One woman brought a curling iron along, perhaps figuring we'd tote a hundred-mile extension cord. Another guest from Michigan couldn't believe that for his nearly $200 per day the best we could manage was to hang a solar shower from a tree. Rather than embracing the unencumbering vitality of the place, many of our passengers fall back on every tiny detail of comfort and service from the outside world, clinging to cold diet caffeine-free sodas and oversized inflatable sleeping pads, and having every last chore taken care of for them. They view their river journey as just another extension of the world they left behind. Several times this summer, kids on my boat exclaimed—after crashing through an exciting rapid—that it was just like Splash Mountain at Disney World. And I had to say, "No. You mean Splash Mountain is just like this."

It's their attitudes as much as their actions that are all twisted and confused. They just don't get it. And many don't want to get it. And we're moving away from even encouraging them to get it. We've eviscerated much of the wildness of these trips in spite of the fact that it is what's most likely to change people and ensure that they have a memorable experience in the wilderness. Instead, we help ensure that our guests completely miss the entire point of where they are and what's possible out there.

Some guides have even reached the extreme conclusion that it's too late for river trips in the U.S. to provide the kinds of experiences they once did. Kurt Wald, who guides down in South America in the off-season, says the beauty of running trips in other countries is that they're still a free-for-all, crazy and unpredictable. He tells a story about how at one company in Costa Rica the guides hijacked all the gear right before a trip and demanded a raise, and the company hired some other guys to go beat them up and steal the gear back. Curt was the T.L. on that trip and he showed up at the put-in with four guides he'd never seen before and had to take a group of clients down a river he'd never seen, either. It was raining and the water was high and he didn't even have a map.

Describing the experience Kurt says, "When you're out there in a situation like that, all you can think about is getting to the take-out. But when you get to the take-out, all you can think about is getting back to the put-in. You think, 'I need another shot of this.' Stuff like that doesn't happen in the States."

Much of the U.S. adventure travel industry has taken to marketing cushy, no-risk trips that emphasize service and minimize anything the least bit challenging or confrontational or that even hints at potentially stretching guests' limits. Outfitters have become in many ways bigger than the wilderness and can overcome its wildness and seem perfectly willing to do so. Once an activity is characterized as being part of the "adventure travel industry" chances are that it's already lost any real vestige of adventure, anyway.

One reason that we've abandoned adventurous trips and replaced them with tame pleasure cruises is that our audience has changed. The kinds of folks who signed up for dory trips fifteen years ago because they wanted to participate in a river expedition are currently looking elsewhere for such experiences. They're running rivers in South America, or scuba diving in Baja, or rock climbing or kayaking or mountain biking—activities where they can participate and revel in the wildness.

Whether it's because the whitewater industry changed its focus to market trips to larger numbers of more sedentary, upscale people, or that these people became attracted to our trips as they naturally became more popular and mainstream and predictable, our typical guest these days is not just rich, but really rich—and accustomed to the kind of service mentality you might encounter at a Four Seasons resort hotel. In the early days, trips were affordable enough that most folks who wanted to experience riding a dory down a pristine river could come up with the means to go.

D.L. has seen the industry and our company go through a lot of changes since his father first founded Grand Canyon Dories and Northwest Dories, and he has a clear perspective on current problems in being successful at the business of adventure. He says, "Getting bigger is good business, but what's being lost isn't being addressed. In the old days we were certainly trying to make some money, but that was not the main goal. You either sacrifice money making, organization, and growing the business in favor of having a special kind of whitewater wilderness experience, or the other way around. I think George Wendt [owner of O.A.R.S.] is caught between a rock and a hard place.

"The experience is different now. Some people are still having magical experiences, but there's so many companies doing this, it's become so professional. Now the competition is who offers the 'best' trip, the best food, the shortest trip, the most convenient. Before, there were no expectations. Now, it's almost like going to the supermarket and picking out your river trip. We have this list of rivers a mile long, which tends to diminish each one. People say, 'Tell me which one is better,' or "Which one can I fit in if I have Thursday off?'"

Of course, in spite of what they might learn from confronting their own limits, some people want a cushy experience in the wilderness. This raises the question of whether we should even accommodate such demands. Pete Gross, one of the classic old-time boatmen who began guiding as a way of communicating to people about environmental issues, questions the very legitimacy of present-day adventure travel.

"Because we want to be there we're willing to be bought," Pete said to me one afternoon as we sat around Boatland and he ate virtually all the leftover trip food in the refrigerator. "People are coming because they want it to be more like Club Med, and maybe those people don't deserve to be here. And maybe I shouldn't be facilitating that experience. In a sense I feel that we're wilderness prostitutes."

Even if some of our guests arrive at the put-in with five-star expectations for a full-service trip, we can trick them into experiencing something wilder, into doing some of the things that will make for a potentially life-altering experience—and we'd be able to accomplish even more if we could just get out of the kitchen. No matter what they envision, once passengers step onto a boat at Corn Creek, they are pretty much ours. Guides can work to present different guests with varying degrees of challenge, and in this way provide wild frontier experiences not only for the wilderness averse, but for more of our adventurous and self-reliant passengers, as well.

D.L. has some more specific advice in this regard. "You set them up by saying, 'Tomorrow's a good Tahiti day,' even when you know they'll have to paddle through Salmon Falls, which is totally safe but has the potential to flip them. The trick is to help them have a semi death-defying experience, but in a safe way, so they really bond, so the trip is memorable. The best trips are the ones where people flip, boats crash, we get flash-flooded. Now with the whole corporate thing you think, 'Oh my God, people could die!' But those are the things that used to make the trips so magical. Guides should get together and not just run the rapids but run the group and steer them toward a particular kind of experience. But that's a high level of responsibility."

It's a tough role for a guide to balance—especially as the industry puts more and more pressure on us to provide service. But it's why many of us are out there. And if we can cause folks to feel things, they'll be more likely to help protect the few such pristine places left to us.

What's frustrating to guides these days is that simply by deciding to come out on the river many folks are bringing themselves close to a life-altering experience, to something powerful and memorable. And yet once they get here, nearly everything we do cushions them from the tough or uncivilized part that makes these places valuable. By bringing the world into the wilderness with us we take away what the place has to offer. By making it too easy for folks we never let them rise to a challenge.

In spite of the neutering of adventure occurring on the Salmon these days, for some folks it can still be a wild place. It may present the highest level of uncertainty and risk they are capable of dealing with. In spite of the changes in the trips and in our core customers, some folks are still experiencing a wilderness adventure on the Salmon, and for them the western myth still survives out there.

The absolutely worst day I spent on the river this season—forty miles along the Road section between the Main and Lower Salmon, during which it poured down cold, sideways rain for nine hours as we rowed against the wind on mostly flat water—was probably the best thing that ever happened to a passenger named Vera. Vera was the kind of person who wore gold and diamonds out on the boats, and asked two women trainees why they'd chosen to pursue such an activity as guiding. Didn't they miss being home with their crystal and china? Vera never would have signed up for a hard-core wilderness trip. One night at dinner she said that if she could come back to this world as anything, she'd choose to be a pampered French poodle (making several of us wish to come back as rolled-up newspapers: *bad* Vera).

Although she considered walking up to the highway that paralleled the river and hitchhiking to the nearest motel; and although she was shivering and miserable all day long, I would guess this was possibly the first time in her life that Vera was tested in such a raw and physical way.

In the face of an unpleasantness beyond the control of any concierge, Vera was forced to call upon reserves of tolerance and good humor I don't think she knew she possessed. At the same time, I believe she was moved by the fact that everyone else on the trip made such an effort to lend her warm clothing and rain gear, and that we stopped for lunch and broke out part of the kitchen to make hot soup for her and the other chilly guests. I'm certain that Vera left the river if not happy about her experience, at least with a far greater sense of her own ability to get through something physically challenging. Of course, at our dinner at Jonathan's following the trip, she still corrected the waitress's wine pouring technique, and insisted on meeting the chef—in spite of our recommendations that she forget this notion—who turned out to be a sixteen-year old girl. But I know that she changed.

It's wonderful to see people like Vera confronting their own frontiers. But, sadly, much of what causes many of our guests to experience backcountry epiphanies these days are such simple and tame actions as sleeping outside, or are caused inadvertently by the few things that are still beyond our control: high water, bad weather, a bear strolling through camp. And it's mostly the guests who've never had any experience in the outdoors before who feel the most powerful wildness on our trips—which still leaves a lot of other folks out. And we need to find a way to keep the myth alive for them, as well.

I think if any of us believed that wildness and all it brings about were not still accessible out on the Salmon, we wouldn't be there rowing and telling stories and encouraging people to hike and paddle and try new things. Of course, many guests do take advantage of this; they do get it. I salute these folks and hope they'll be on my next trip.

But for the others, for guests like Rita—a hugely overweight woman who refused to drink the beer she'd craved all day because it wasn't cold enough, and who complained about a fleck of dirt in the hand-whipped cream on her strawberry shortcake—I say, with all due respect and every good intention: get off your lazy fat ass and participate. Take a walk along the beach around the next river bend some evening instead of reading a Steven King novel and drinking too much and complaining that you're tired when all you've done all day is sit on the boat and eat.

I say, for your own good and with great hope and encouragement: bravely venture into the kitchen and slice a zucchini. Offer to help pack a boat, or insist on rowing one. Climb into an inflatable kayak. Wake up early and sit in a quiet place and listen to the river, or stay up late and watch for shooting stars. Perhaps you'll be treated to the sight of a moose swimming across the current, or a mountain sheep sipping from a deep pool. Or maybe the color of the light as it dusts the tops of the trees will make your heart ache, or transport you back to childhood, or just make you feel.

There are a thousand moments to grasp out along the river, untold wild things you can do that you may never have the chance to do again. Take a risk with someone you love, or someone you just met. Let the wilderness act on you. Wail and undulate crazily by the water's edge. Stand barefoot in a side creek until your feet go numb. Your guides wish nothing more than to help you with these things but we may be too busy baking a peach cobbler at five A.M. So wake up and listen to your heart; it's pounding to a rhythm that is your life, a rhythm that can move you to run or cry out or embrace the nervous passenger next to you. Swim across the river, or walk across the bottom by carrying a huge rock. Play goofily. Haul yourself up on the trail and hug trees just to smell their vanilla perfume. Collect pine boughs for a fire or wildflowers for a centerpiece or anecdotes for a story to tell as you sit around in the evening.

These are just some of the places where adventure dwells. These are just some of the places where wildness resides. Get in touch with it. Make this trip, the world, your life, something beautiful and original and all your own. Put down your cell phone, put up your own tent, do something—anything—for the love of God!

And beneath a lingering dusk on a hot, dry August evening, when you're standing under the water-clear sky above camp as the light purples and stars pop out; or later, in darkness, when the fire gives off the stored heat and sweet scent of yellow pine and the smoke drifts fragrantly up toward the rim of the canyon, and bats flitter restlessly, and the moon begins its slow rise with a rich orange glow beyond a distant ridge; when the stillness balances with the whispering, riffling rush of whitewater and you're lying in the cool sand by the warm coals with a group of new friends, and the dories are pulled up on the beach, you may understand—perhaps for just a few perfect moments, when no one speaks—what wilderness is worth.

As your own life rolls past like the endless water of the river, flowing by and yet remaining constant; as your companions sigh and lie back looking at the spilled crystals of stars scattered across the sky, open yourself to wildness and you may finally understand what it all means, what's here for you, and why you've come.

Games

> *"The way of the gamesman is hard, his training strict, his progress slow, his disappointments many."*
> STEPHEN POTTER, *THE THEORY AND PRACTICE OF GAMESMANSHIP*

Killer Goat Beach, on the Lower Salmon, may well comprise the best baseball stadium on the entire river. Known for many years as Packers Creek Camp, the BLM first officially printed the more evocative name on its 1995 river maps. I was riding in the crew cab with Joel on the way to the put-in one day when somebody mentioned the change on the new map. I never saw Joel light up like that before or since. Killer Goat Beach was named after an incident in which he was the undisputed co-star, along with a feral goat.

You really have to hear Joel tell the story, hear him describe various people "coming unGLUED" to appreciate it, but here, at least, are the details: when one of Joel's trips was camping on this beach a few years ago, a feral goat stood on some rocks above camp, watching them. One of the guests on this trip was "a fitness nut," and after pitching his tent in the sand high up the beach, he began doing stretching exercises, which inexplicably upset the goat. Joel, who was working in the kitchen, noticed the goat's agitation and asked the man to stop, but he refused. After a few more minutes the man began jogging laps around his tent, which really irritated the goat, and though several other guides suggested he quit it, the man still refused. Shortly after that the goat charged, and as it chased the man in a circle Joel yelled at him, "Stay away from the kitchen! Stay away from the kitchen!" So the man headed directly for the kitchen, with the goat in hot pursuit.

Joel stood beside one of the prep tables as the man ran past him, but the goat just stopped and lowered his head and he and Joel had a long face-off. After a minute or two of staring at Joel, the goat finally charged again. Joel picked up a piece of wood lying on a nearby table, swung it like a baseball bat, and smacked the goat right between the eyes. Nobody can replicate Joel's lanky imitation of the stunned goat staggering and falling to its knees before retreating drunkenly back up the beach.

Following this incident, several different outfitters reported to the BLM that while camping at Packers Creek their groups were attacked by a crazy killer goat. The goat earned such a fabulous reputation that when a couple of BLM bigshots from Washington were visiting the Salmon River a few years ago, local rangers motored them to the beach in the hope that the lunatic goat might make an appearance. While they were standing on the bow of their government jet boat, the goat not only showed himself: he charged the rangers like an angered plains buffalo. One of them pulled out a gun and—supposedly in self-defense—put an end to the terror of Killer Goat Beach.

It's a pleasure to hear Joel—who is not a showman like some guides—tell this story without self-consciousness and describe his own role in modern Salmon River history. None of which has anything to do with the fact that Killer Goat Beach—long, wide, and flat—constitutes the best baseball venue along the entire river. A few days before we ran The Slide Rapid on this Lower

Salmon trip, we made camp at Killer Goat Beach during the hottest part of a blistering afternoon. Before we'd even begun unloading the boats, Leon began talking about having a baseball game.

In spite of the heat, we cajoled about half a dozen guests—men, women, and children—into playing under the glaring sun in the burning sand. We began a bit lethargically, but as we got into it I noticed that even the adults—especially the adults, and even more especially the adult males—were starting to take things a little more seriously. For one thing, everybody seemed to be keeping score.

Two of the players were Tom, a large, slightly-menacing physician from Tacoma, Washington, and Stew, a distinguished-looking prep school teacher from Pennsylvania who sported a brand-new, dapper, white beard. Late in the game, with the score tied, Stew roped a line drive up the middle that got him to second base. Although the next batter struck out, the hitter after him knocked a lame-duck Texas-leaguer just over Tom's head where he was playing first. Stew took off for third base as Tom struggled in the sand to go after the ball. He picked it up just as Stew arrived at third.

The two men considered each other across the white-hot sand of the infield in much the same way that Joel and the killer goat probably took measure of one another in that earlier, ill-fated confrontation. They weighed their options, each waiting for the other to make a move. Stew took a tentative step off third base, and Tom edged a little closer toward home. When something snapped in Stew's brain and shouted at him to JUST GO!, Tom reacted instantly, too, and both men ran as fast as they could in the heavy sand toward the plate—a race that progressed in slow, exaggerated motion. When it appeared that they were destined to collide in a perfect tie, and that one or the other of them must back off, Stew thought he saw his chance and *dove* toward home plate, leaping head-first through the air in a manner that would have made Pete Rose proud. Not to be outdone, Tom saw that he'd have to dive, as well, and without a second thought he launched himself toward home. The two men crashed head-on in midair, fell to the ground, rolled around in a heap, and came up coughing, laughing, and spitting sand.

Although boatmen present virtually unlimited examples of arrested development, it's always entertaining to watch otherwise normal adults acting so much like children. This baseball game stands out as one of my favorite moments from the summer because you could actually see each of these men as little kids. In the backcountry, we often fail to consider how things look or what other folks might say; we don't measure our actions against what's appropriate behavior for a lawyer or a doctor or a CEO. Instead, we turn virtually every activity into some kind of a game. It is part of the unlimited freedom provided by our kindly host, the wilderness.

A hundred examples of this occur every day. At lunch, once we've set up the peanut butter bar and the water pump and lugged a few of the heavier items up on shore, we guides return to our boats to pull lunch food out of coolers and rocket boxes, at which point it's requisite to throw these items—blocks of cheese, stalks of celery, tomatoes, fruit, boxes of cookies—from the boats up to the lunch table one at a time, preferably just fast enough to make them difficult to catch. There's no real objective; it's just that we so rarely have an opportunity to really chuck a tomato or wing a carrot back home, so we take advantage of these circumstances. Contrary to what my mother might say, I've never seen anybody lose an eye to a bag of Fig Newtons.

Or consider the breakfast item/ritual known as "drop zone

eggs." Once the griddle has really heated up, a guide—preferably a tall one, or one standing on a bucket, or a light one sitting on the shoulders of another guide—holds an egg as high above the griddle as possible, and then cracks it so that the egg wobbles down through space and then splatters on the hot surface, cooking instantly. In the advanced version of this game, two participants put on hot-gloves and protective kayaking helmets and hold the griddle up between them like a strike zone while someone else runs down the beach and then pitches fastball eggs at the sizzling target.

Only actual children like to play in the kitchen more than boatmen do. Among the most entertaining kitchen-related games are the amazing pyrotechnics produced, for example, by stuffing a bunch of steel wool into a metal can poked full of holes, attaching a long string to the can, rowing the whole thing out on a dory into a big eddy at night, then lighting it on fire and swinging it around on the string. On a dark evening these poorman's fireworks release dazzling wheels of white sparks against the pitch-black horizon.

Many guides also aspire to create the largest grease bomb ever ignited on the river—which involves saving up sausage and bacon grease and the drippings from grilled steaks in an empty tin can over the course of an entire trip. On the final night, just after we give out awards to all our guests—Most Likely to Become a Boatman, for example, or The Mark Spitz Award (usually given to someone who fell out of a boat in a rapid and survived a harrowing swim that we can now joke about)—one guide slips down to the river and dons a wet suit for maximum protection against splattering grease and flames, and using a long pole lowers the can of grease by means of a wire handle into the middle of a roaring fire.

When the grease has begun boiling and smoking, the guide takes another can full of cold river water and using the pole again, pours the water into the burning grease—something we seriously advise against trying at home. A good grease bomb looks a lot like those films you've seen of nuclear testing, if on a slightly smaller scale. Of course, since grease bombs are dangerous as well as illegal along the Salmon River, I've only heard about them, and have never actually seen one in person. I've certainly never seen a guide who, for the sake of anonymity I'll call "Robert," ignite a series of amazing grease and margarine bombs right by the river's edge at the bottom of French Creek Camp on the night of the Fourth of July.

Many old-time boatmen also revere a game which involves seeing how fast a rookie can set up the roll-top table, a kind of clumsy gear puzzle that many trainees try to avoid dealing with altogether. This year, when Trista was unable to put the table together on land in under one minute, Leon encouraged her to try it while standing in the river so the water could help her balance the table top while she tried to attach it to the legs. Chris Quinn claims to hold the record for assembling the table in under seven seconds, but the most amazing part of his feat was that he'd remembered to bring the table at all.

On trips where we've brought along a paddle raft, we sometimes flip the empty boat upside down in camp and set it on a piece of beach that slopes precipitously toward a deep spot in an eddy. A boatman stands on each side of the raft with a bucket and tosses river water onto the bottom to slick down the surface, creating a sixteen-foot "Slip-n-Slide." There's nothing quite like the spectacle of a retired lawyer from Seattle running down the beach in her frumpy bathing suit, leaping headlong across the bottom of the raft, and disappearing into the river in such a way that for a moment only her feet are visible before they, too, disappear over the edge of the boat; or the sight of a portly, gravel-voiced businessman from Chicago showing off for his daughter by performing a giant belly-flop on the Slip-n-Slide and bouncing into the river.

Guides also possess a limitless repertoire of verbal games for passing long afternoons rowing against the wind on flat water, or for playing around the fire in the evening. Minute mysteries provide a foolproof way of spending a slow hour or two on the boats, and are perfect for quieting down unruly kids. For example: a naked woman is lying dead at the bottom of a mountain with a match stick in her hand. You can ask me "yes" or "no" questions to determine what happened.

Some of our evening games also provide a great way for trip participants to get to know each other and begin bonding. Leon often leads a game called "Two Truths and a Lie" on the first night of a trip. The game requires players to offer three brief statements or stories about themselves to the rest of the group; as you may have already guessed, two are true, one is a lie. The stated object is for the storyteller to try and fool everybody else, but the real purpose is to give each group member a moment in the spotlight, and provide them with a means of introducing themselves in some entertaining way. My own stories often included the following:

— that I received a speeding ticket while taking my first drivers' test;
— that in college I was a nationally-ranked croquet player;
— that I once had an out-of-body experience.

After the season was over, I spoke to Sandra Gaskill about the trip we worked on together that included guests (and baseball legends) Tom and Stew, as well as guides Joel, Leon, and Brannon. We both agreed that this was one of the best groups we'd encountered all summer, and I asked her why she thought this had been so.

"It had a lot to do with that first night, when we sat around and played two truths and a lie," Sandra said. "That really set a tone and people felt they were in an environment that was comfortable, and they pushed themselves, and grew."

Strange and magical things occur when two dozen folks sit around a fire on a sparkling clear evening and sip drinks and tell stories and play such games as Smurf and Aardvark; Elves, Wizards, and Dwarves; or In the Manner of the Word. But it's hard to explain. You'll just have to come out there with us and experience it for yourself.

Is there a point to all of this? Is play somehow a metaphor for how our primordial instinct to have fun emerges fresh and wild when we step away from all the serious and mundane rules of society? Is there a deeper, hidden meaning—an undercurrent or subtext or inner frontier—to these games? And would Frederick Jackson Turner have taken his turn on the Slip-n-Slide?

In answer, all I can say is that if you thought I was going to reveal how the naked dead woman ended up at the bottom of the mountain with a match in her hand, you've got another think coming.

The Unit

> *"The unit is no arena for jokes. There is nothing funny about the unit."*
> KURT WALD, RIVER GUIDE

Kurt Wald likes to begin his unit talk by reminding passengers—only half kidding—that they'll be sorry if they don't pay close attention. He adopts an attitude of cool professionalism, like a surgeon explaining a delicate procedure.

Brannon, on the other hand, delivers his unit talk—sitting on it through most of the live simulation—like a stand-up comic hitting his stride. He rests his feet, knees high, on the edge of the tank that flares out beneath the seat, and pulls up on the two strap handles on the sides so that he looks like a little kid in the crash position. He explains that in the case of a flash flood you could assume this posture and ride down river using the unit as flotation. He demonstrates high-siding the unit in case it's been set on sloping or uneven ground.

Barry, a renowned anal retentive, strictly lectures on the "Three P's": no peeing (there's a separate bucket for this, or you should do it in the river); no paper (there are separate cans for new and used paper, the latter of which we empty every day); and no parking (very important on a trip with thirty people and one unit).

I like to begin my own unit talk with a little history, stress with utter seriousness the guests' responsibilities in regard to the unit, and then introduce a little levity. All of which is to say that somehow the unit talk has become a vehicle for the expression of personal style.

The unit actually goes by many names. Early commercial river outfitters called it "The Groover" because they employed a metal army surplus rocket box, which imprinted two grooves from the edges of the box on your butt after you got up. Some folks refer to the unit as "The Growler," due to the noises your stomach may broadcast during a visit, but this is a somewhat archaic term. Today we use a dark green plastic box with an attachable toilet seat, and sometimes refer to it fondly as "The Green Machine." But most of us opt for the elegance and simplicity of: the unit.

We have adopted many clever systems to ensure that the entire unit experience is private, comfortable, and hygienic. We've even developed a neat way of indicating whether it's currently in use: we place a kayak paddle at the head of the unit trail where it leads out of camp. When approaching the facility, you take the paddle with you. So if you see it leaning against a tree by the trail head, you know there's a vacancy.

To promote proper hygiene, we also provide running water by placing a bucketful of river on a flat rock. Beside it, we set a container of biodegradable hand soap and a tin can with a hole poked in the side near the bottom, and a wire loop protruding from the top. Fill the can with water, hang it from the edge of the bucket, and water streams out through the hole as out of a faucet. High tech in the wilderness.

Although we try to emphasize that folks shouldn't linger, and in spite of the fact that reading material is prohibited, we do encourage everyone to relax and enjoy the view. We usually set up the unit in the privacy of a copse of trees or behind the camouflage of boulders away from camp, and frequently above camp, too. So it may very well feature striking vistas of beaches, rapids, and occasionally a downstream panorama. Certainly it will be among the most scenic spots most of our guests have ever enjoyed while pursuing this particular activity.

On the first evening of a new trip, when we present guests with a thousand details about the kitchen, how to set up their tents, and what dangers to look out for—rattlesnakes, poison oak, flash floods—many people seem most engaged, mesmerized even, by the unit talk. Passengers exchange the kinds of glances I would imagine passing between novice sky divers as they look around the plane.

A lot of passengers actually think we're kidding about carrying this thing around with us for a week; other folks take notice of which boat is carrying the green box and avoid riding there. When we explain that since hundreds of people camp in the same spots every summer and if we buried our waste there'd be no place left to sleep, some people seem like they'd be willing to make that compromise. Over the years I've had several passengers on shorter trips who claimed to have held out for three or four days without going at all. You see these folks smiling tightly at meals and munching on a leaf of lettuce or a carrot stick, gazing longingly at the salmon steaks sizzling on the grill.

Many great stories have grown up around the unit—fertilized by it, you might say. On one trip late in the season I spotted an elderly guest named Walt walking there in the early morning with a cigar in one hand and a bottle full of pee in the other. A woman named Corinne was startled by a porcupine during a nighttime reconnoiter; while we were sitting around the campfire we heard her screams and peered into the darkness in alarm. Joel said it was probably just someone encountering a porcupine while on the unit, and he went back to sipping his Bushmill's when no other distress calls ensued. On another trip, three middle-aged men from the Midwest created a sport out of trying to snap each other's photos while they were parked. They took to employing spouses and children as decoys to try to draw away the photographer's attention when they were moved to pay a visit. A jolly guest named Irwin came running into the kitchen one morning in triumph with his camera, having staked out the site by hiding behind a nearby tree and waiting for his old friend Buddy to sneak up there when he thought the coast was clear.

But my very favorite unit story involves an old codger guide named Casey, who spends much of his time reminding other guides how experienced he is, and how green they are. He sounds like a crusty old pirate when he says, "Arghh...I've been doin' this for FIFTEEN YEARS and I've never seen anyone chop an onion like that." Or crack an egg. Or tie a knot. Or clear their throat.

So when he and Nikki and Remony were breaking down the unit one morning and lugging it back to the boats, neither of the others had the nerve to ask Casey why he was risking carrying the unit tank by its lid, rather than by the handles—a daring stunt. I only wish I'd been lucky enough to witness the container disconnecting from the lid, which stayed in Casey's hand. The container hit the ground with the full weight of its toxic contents, which exploded out the top, splashing Casey and sending him into a sprint for the river. Nobody had seen him move that fast in several decades.

For some very strange reason, the unit makes a lasting impression on people, and they talk about it almost fondly after the trip, the way you might reminisce about the worst cab ride you ever had, or the time your luggage got sent to Bora Bora when you were headed for Walla Walla.

Along the Fault Line: Fractures in the Myth

"Now occurred that great epoch in the Lewis-Clark Expedition—an event which helped shape the future destinies of the United States and makes Sacajawea stand out as the one woman—be she white, red, yellow, or black—who did the most outstanding thing to change the whole future of the peoples of the North American continent.

"...the writer...unhesitatingly makes the assertion, without fear of successful contradiction, that if Cameawhait and his people had deserted Lewis and Clark at the time Sacajawea pleaded for the continuation of his assistance, the Lewis and Clark expedition would never have crossed the mountains and lived to tell the tale. Had they failed, the entire map and history of the United States would have been vastly different from what it is today. Search American history where I may, I can find no record of achievement by a woman which has had such a profound bearing on the destinies of the nation."
ROBERT G. BAILEY, *RIVER OF NO RETURN*

"I like to think I can do anything—maybe not the same way as a man, but I like to think there aren't any restrictions because I'm a woman."
SANDRA GASKILL, RIVER GUIDE

"[Historians] turned the tables and chronicled what they perceived as inequalities and injustices suffered by the hitherto 'forgotten

people' on the frontier—Indians, blacks, Hispanics, and women. In a similarly negative vein—and reflecting contemporary environmental concerns—a growing number of scholars severely criticized the ravishing of the natural environment by successive generations of westerners. To a considerable extent, then, historians were finding the frontier responsible for what they considered to be major ills... racism, inequality, and the wanton destruction of nature."
GERALD NASH, *CREATING THE WEST*

The historian T.A. Larson has noted a particularly interesting sentence in Frederick Jackson Turner's famous essay, *The Significance of the Frontier in American History*. The sentence reads: "Kit Carson's mother was a Boone."

While not exactly scintillating on its own, Larson points out that this sentence constitutes the only reference to a woman in the entire essay.

At least during the early days of western exploration, women comprised a very small minority of the population beyond the Rocky Mountains. According to Carrey and Conley, at one time men outnumbered women by more than fifty to one along the Salmon River—a nonetheless isolated statistic which doesn't quite explain Turner's neglect of the entire gender. Turner's frontier thesis and the myth that grew up with and out of it still exclude thousands of women who worked alongside their men, or solo, in civilizing their own portions of the frontier.

In 1870, the census documented nearly 200,000 women over the age of twenty-one living in the West. Their numbers alone suggest that their apparent insignificance in early academic history—and in the mythology of the American frontier—has more to do with who wrote that history than it does with reality. A better explanation of why women seem AWOL from many accounts of the early West might contend that regardless of their actual role in settling the frontier, few women worked as historians a century ago, and that both history and the mythical West were created by, for, and about men—and white men, at that.

In the past couple of decades, Turner's thesis has taken some serious hits, many of them from a modern school of historians who created the concept of the "New West" to correct misconceptions that the frontier was all about brave, handsome white men conquering the wilderness and relishing the task the way a hotshot gunfighter relishes high noon. Among other goals, New West historians sought to expand the narrow view of the West by acknowledging and celebrating the contributions and experiences of women, blacks, Native Americans, and other minorities. These historians also sought to show that everything about the western frontier was not as boastfully positive and ruggedly delightful as Turner implied.

Unfortunately, while scholars have worked hard in academic circles to emend many misconceptions about the frontier, nobody has performed a similar repair job to correct the glaring omissions and limitations of the popular western myth. In fact, the general public has continued to embrace this narrow, romanticized version of the West. As the historian James B. Grossman, says in an introduction to *The Frontier in American Culture*, "...most academics had relegated [Turner] to the periphery years ago... The frontier thesis in the minds of reporters, and apparently their readers, remains vital. It persists as the standard explanation of western and American exceptionalism. It remains so deeply embedded in a wider constellation of images about the West and the United States that the reporters regard any questioning of it as radical and daring."

Many folks who've never heard of Frederick Jackson Turner may be drawn to undertake a week-long trip on the Salmon

River at least partly by a vague notion of a frontier similar to the mythical one Turner helped popularize. Yet these passengers will necessarily encounter evidence throughout their journeys that contradicts various aspects of the myth—which provides an excellent opportunity for a little renovation. Such evidence might present itself the moment they show up at the put-in and realize that half of their river guides are women. Seeing women working as river guides may also shatter some of their perfectly modern prejudices and misconceptions that have nothing at all to do with the frontier.

Thanks to Carrey and Conley's *River of No Return* we know that women—many of whom were no doubt as ruggedly individualistic as their male counterparts—comprised an integral component of pioneer life along the Salmon River in the early years of settlement, after the almost exclusively male population of gold miners wandered off somewhere else in search of another lode. Even so, these women lived outside the limited focus of Turnerism and the western myth. Likewise, although women river guides are no more unusual than were women pioneers, and since river guides are heirs to the mythical western archetype—outdoorsy, individualistic, rugged, etc.—recognizing women as a part of this community also necessarily challenges the western myth. For women, working as river guides on the modern frontier of the Salmon River may present a sort of frontier in itself.

Of course, to women guides the entire context of American western mythology may seem silly, patronizing, or irrelevant. But this is dangerous terrain, and an excellent place to avoid assumptions—which is why I decided to ask one of my fellow guides what she thought about the whole thing.

I am still in trouble with Trista because I told her I was curious to hear a woman's perspective on working along the river. We were sitting on the deck of a dory parked out behind Boatland on a hot afternoon. Trista smiled sadly and shook her head. "You don't just want to hear my perspective as a guide?" she said. "It has to be as a woman guide? That's so lame."

Trista, at twenty-three, is nothing if not sure of herself. She claimed that for her this "issue" of women guides was not an issue at all. She thought the very fact that I suggested women's experiences on the river were different from men's made me sexist. Dangerous terrain, indeed.

Although she seemed to wish that I'd shut up and move on to a more interesting topic, Trista was admittedly troubled by an aspect of the relationship between the sexes out on the river, and by some peoples' reactions to women guides. What seemed to be at the root of her discomfort was the fact that some folks were surprised to see women working as guides and didn't know how to respond or accept it, because that's not the kind of thing the myth—or some current attitudes toward women—prepared them for. As Trista explained rather passionately:

"Sexism prevents some people from benefiting from having women on a river trip. On my last trip there was a guy who had a fly-fishing rod and he was totally inept. He could cast, but he didn't know how to read water and he didn't know where the fish were. I kept telling him that I knew how to fly fish and that I'd been down the river a couple of times and that I knew a couple of places to fish. I pointed out a couple of holes and said right behind that rock or that rock there'd probably be some big fish. I knew they were there, and I knew a lot of the insects that were flying around and probably the right flies that were working. He was all off; he caught maybe one fish the whole trip. To go on a Main Salmon trip and catch one fish—what a goon.

"And so Lonnie was helping him out and I thought it was so odd that he could take Lonnie's advice so easily, but whenever I would suggest something he would totally discount it and he wouldn't follow my advice. It was frustrating."

At the very least, the western myth, and the perception of reality in the shadow of the myth, contains a major flaw, especially if river guides are among its current archetypes, and guides include women: some people just can't reconcile their romantic images of the frontier (or, for that matter, the present) with reality. What Trista interpreted as sexism has roots in the exclusionary view of Turner, and in the myth that his theories inspired.

Sandra Gaskill also acknowledges these problems, but sees river trips as a great way of shattering misconceptions promulgated by the myth and making the myth itself, as well as current views of women, more inclusive. In Sandra's opinion, women guides can provide a positive experience for both men and women passengers not just by being great guides, but by the very fact that they are women. Sandra described doing exactly that: "On the Boy Scout trip, one boy made a sexist comment, and I threw him in the river. The scouts thought I was a radical feminist so they were trying to get my goat. But they were just being boys and testing the waters. One of the coolest things for me was that we could banter and play. They talked to me about feminism; they wanted to know what it was, and was I really a feminist. A few got into an intellectual discussion about feminism and what it meant, and I gave them feedback about their actions. I thought, 'Wow, these are twelve- to fifteen-year old kids seeing a woman in a nontraditional role.' That was really good."

D.L. likes working with women for this same reason: they help folks get beyond the limitations of the myth. He says, "I appreciate women guides because they make this less of a machismo thing that you have to be a half mountain man to guide river trips, so we can get off that and appreciate the place for what it is."

In addition to debunking the exclusionary nature of the myth, Sandra felt that women guides could inspire other women to act in ways that contradict the traditional roles they've so often been cast in. She described her relationship with one particular passenger, a single mother who seemed a bit lost in the world: "Cynthia thought it was fantastic that women were getting out and being adventurous and hiking and rafting, and she wished that she'd had that kind of experience. At the end of the trip she decided she was going to take her son on a ten-day backpacking trip. Seeing a woman doing some of that helped her to have confidence in herself."

Still, myths are elusive and resilient, and they die hard. In an essay entitled "The Adventures of the Frontier in the Twentieth Century," Patricia Limerick Nelson, a gifted New West historian, writes with great humor and insight about the folly of the frontier myth at the same time that she marvels at its ability to survive in light of all the sensible evidence that disproves it. Nelson says, "As a mental artifact, the frontier has demonstrated an astonishing stickiness and persistence. It is virtually the flypaper of our mental world; it attaches itself to everything—healthful diets, space shuttles, civil rights campaigns, heart transplants, industrial product development, musical innovations. Packed full of nonsense and goofiness, jammed with nationalistic self-congratulations and toxic ethnocentrism, the image of the frontier is nonetheless universally recognized and laden with positive associations... The concept works as a cultural glue—a mental and emotional fastener that, in some very curious and unexpected ways, works to hold us together."

We cling to our myths for good reason: they comfort and inspire us; they help us to believe that a better place and time lies just beyond the horizon. Regardless of how imprecise, narrow-minded, and idealized the western myth has always been, we sorely need it, particularly as the West grows too civilized and the frontier recedes so far that we can barely make out its silhouette against the western sky. We need the myth and its accompanying concepts of Americans as resourceful, independent, strong-willed, and rugged. We need to believe that new frontiers still await us out in some distant wilderness, even if only in some wilderness of the heart.

Why destroy these beautiful and useful notions that we so love just because they are inaccurate? Why not simply expand our myths to be more inclusive? The myth's treatment of women is only one place where it exhibits flaws, but why not doctor the damaged parts and ride these bucking, sometimes-ornery notions as far as they can take us?

Native Americans

"A proper understanding of the Indian problem encountered at mid-nineteenth century in the Pacific Northwest requires a review of American Indian policies after the colonial era. Every student is aware of the oft repeated cycle governing white and Indian relations: A council was held and a treaty made; Indians ceded lands in return for presents and for promised annuities; boundary lines were marked and declared inviolable. Peace lasted a few years but was destroyed by the encroachment of settlers who crossed the line to hunt, prospect, graze stock, and farm. These invasions brought protests, massacres, battles, and ultimately victory to the troops. Then a new treaty was made, and the cycle inevitably operated upon the next frontier."
MERRILL BEAL, *I WILL FIGHT NO MORE FOREVER*

"The whites told only one side. Told it to please themselves. Told much that is not true. Only his own best deeds, only the worst deeds of the Indians, has the white man told."
YELLOW WOLF OF THE NEZ PERCE TRIBE

Just before the entrance to deep, narrow Green Canyon in the Lower Gorge, a weathered old homesteader's cabin marks the site of Shorts Bar on river right. Beyond a small eddy, the river turns and the current piles into the sheer right wall and then pillows back upon itself. As we're tying up our boats to some rocks on shore here, a gang of loud teenagers in inflatable kayaks paddles around the corner above us. Some of them aim for the eddy, while others head downstream. One boater can't decide which of his friends to follow; he floats past and drifts into the wall and flips.

We encountered this group earlier in the trip, and we're not especially glad to see them again. Yesterday, as we rowed past their camp, they shouted at us to keep an eye out for a boat they'd lost. Now their leaders—fat, red-faced men wearing camouflage tee-shirts and paddling a small four-man raft with their legs straddling the tubes and their feet dangling in the water—yell conflicting commands at each other. Somehow they manage to surge into the eddy, where they begin screaming at all the other boats going past that this is Shorts Bar! Shorts Bar!, where the Indian pictographs (one genius calls them "the injun pictures") are located.

A couple of the young kayakers who've bumped into my dory without a word of apology, and who now hang on my gunwale to keep from drifting, look at each other and roll their eyes.

"Big fucking deal," the first one says, referring to the pictographs.

"We don't need no steen-king pictographs," the other one says, in a fake Mexican accent, and they laugh and paddle back out into the current, grazing the canyon wall on the right and nearly flipping before they disappear down river.

In the course of the last few millennia, various groups of Native Americans lived along or visited the Salmon River. We know that ancestors of several tribes inhabited the area around Corn Creek approximately 8000 years ago, and that Mountain Sheepeater Shoshone made winter camps at Mackay Bar in the eighteenth century. We know that the Nez Perce welcomed Lewis and Clark and helped the explorers on their journey west, and that a party of these Indians even escorted Captain Clark down the Salmon fourteen miles past North Fork in 1805.

Although archaeological data attests to an early and long-term Native American presence, and the historical accounts of explorers, settlers, and miners describe interactions with friendly natives (as well as hostile ones) in the Salmon River country, to-day folks on a wilderness river trip are unlikely to encounter more than the vaguest evidence that these were sacred home-lands and busy fishing grounds for several tribes for thousands of years. Plenty of settlers' cabins built in the last century adorn the river banks (Shorts Bar was named for a recent white resident, not for the natives who left their marks here so much earlier), but almost no traces remain to remind travelers of the folks who for eons called this country home. Only an occasional figure etched or painted on stone—such as the set of drawings just downstream of the cabin on Shorts Bar—survives.

That a group of boys ignored some of the subtle, infrequent signs that do exist, reinforces the pattern of indifference and even hostility with which the majority of whites have reacted to most anything Native American for nearly two hundred years. Not incidentally, Native Americans—along with women, blacks, and other minorities—lived largely outside of the narrow and flawed focus of early frontier history promulgated by Frederick Jackson Turner and the myth of the American West. Where ac-counts from these schools of thought did include America's original residents, they usually depicted the natives in an off-handed or one-dimensional manner. New West scholars have been working hard to correct the limited view of history in this regard, leaving the rest of us with the opportunity to renovate and expand flawed notions of the western myth.

The Indian tales we have inherited often describe white settlers subduing bellicose natives in the process of civilizing the frontier. Such events—whether true or invented—make for dramatic storytelling. But portraying Indians from this limited perspective discounts their own experiences in the West and attaches them as a tangential part of the exclusionary tale of white men blazing jauntily toward the Pacific.

One of the few stories about Indians along the Salmon River that survives in popular circles concerns Chief Joseph and the Nez Perce War—a perfect western story from the white American point of view because it depicts a tribe of noble Indians who fought valiantly until the might and Manifest Destiny of the United States subdued them. The Chief Joseph story may also be so popular—you can pick up a book about him in nearly any cafe or outfitter's office in central and western Idaho—because it is the last story about Indians along the Salmon River. As happened with the frontier itself after folks realized it might actually be gone, people began to embrace and admire Chief Joseph only after the army removed him to a safe distance, only after he lived on in the mythical rather than the actual West.

The Nez Perce War occurred in 1877, but the trouble that caused it began long before then. You could say it started the day Lewis and Clark departed from Missouri nearly three quarters of a century earlier to explore the West—or even when the pilgrims first landed at Plymouth Rock.

During the decades that our ancestors were settling the continent, our government laid the groundwork for the tragedy that befell Chief Joseph's tribe by making a series of treaties with some—but not all—of the Nez Perce leaders. The so-called "treaty Nez Perce," who believed that the white men would really leave them alone once they pulled all of the gold from the ground, or once they'd passed through to the Pacific, ceded tracts of land in exchange for gifts, money, and guarantees that most of their wide-ranging homeland would remain theirs in perpetuity. But subsequent generations of miners, settlers, and politicians continually demanded or simply took just a little more land. Following a long history of broken treaties—which the Nez Perce abided with patience and good faith—the government finally requested that the entire tribe, including those who never signed any treaties ceding anything, leave their homeland and move to the Lapwai Reservation in Idaho.

Although the treaty Nez Perce agreed, several other "non-treaty" bands, including Chief Joseph's, resisted. Finally, in the late spring of 1877, General Oliver Howard issued an ultimatum for the Indians to gather their stock, pack their belongings, and move from the land that had been promised to them forever—land that they'd always lived on and loved as their mother—in thirty days, although doing so would require them to cross the Salmon and Snake Rivers, which were at flood stage and therefore extremely dangerous. At this time, even Joseph and the other non-treaty Nez Perce agreed to comply, because they did not want to go to war. Joseph ultimately believed that if only they'd been given enough time to gather their far-flung herds and move without duress, there would have been no fighting.

Explanations regarding exactly what precipitated the war vary slightly, but the facts seem to indicate that a couple of young Indians—fed up with years of white abuse, having their stock stolen, and the pressure of the sudden move—took revenge at this volatile time on a couple of white men who were known to have murdered Indians. Settlers were appalled and demanded protection, and the army responded with force.

Just a few miles from the Salmon up White Bird Creek, troops under the command of Captain David Perry attacked the Nez Perce, even though—according to at least one account—several Indians approached them waving a white flag. The tribe's warriors defended themselves with great skill and inflicted heavy casualties on the troops without losing a single man of their own. The battle has since been compared to Custer's demise at Little Big Horn.

Following the White Bird fight, the Indians held council and decided they'd better flee because more soldiers would surely come for them. Joseph crossed and recrossed the Salmon several times at high water—with women, children, old folks, and stock animals—led his people over the mountains, and executed brilliant maneuvers to evade and occasionally inflict losses upon the army units pursuing him. At first, the Indians believed they were safe when they crossed over into Montana, figuring that their dispute was with the white men in Idaho. But when soldiers continued the chase, the Indians kept moving. Over the next eleven weeks the Nez Perce engaged ten separate American military commands in thirteen battles across approximately 1600 miles of difficult terrain. The exhausted Indians were finally forced to surrender just forty miles from the Canadian border, where they had stopped to rest, thinking they were finally home free.

Chief Joseph was later to say that he only surrendered because he believed Colonel Nelson Miles' promise that the army would return Joseph's people to the Lapwai Reservation in Idaho, not far from their homeland. On October 5, he told Miles in a now-famous speech: "I am tired of fighting. Our Chiefs are killed... The old men are all killed... It is cold and we have no blankets. The little children are freezing to death. My people, some of them, have run away to the hills and have no blankets, no food; no one knows where they are, perhaps freezing to death. I want time to look for my children and see how many of them I can find. Maybe I shall find them among the dead. Hear me, my chiefs, I am tired; my heart is sick and sad. From where the sun now stands, I will fight no more forever."

When the army shipped the Nez Perce off to a reservation in Oklahoma, not Idaho (against Colonel Miles' pleas that the government honor his promise) following the war, the American government had succeeded in destroying an essential element of the original frontier that we as a nation have always needed so desperately to define ourselves. Throughout western history the presence of Indians has been one more way of characterizing that frontier: as long as there were free-ranging Native Americans to fear and mistreat, the frontier existed; once they'd been subdued, pushed off the land, killed by alcohol or smallpox or war, the frontier had been civilized. The end of the Nez Perce war marked the end of Indians along the Salmon River, and the close of that particular aspect of the frontier—except where it continued to thrive in myth.

There's plenty more to the story of Chief Joseph and the Nez Perce. Leon often delivers a compelling version of the tale around the fire in camp, complete with visual aids such as river pebbles and pine cones representing the various army and Indian units, and piles of sand representing mountain ranges and maybe a rope to stand for the river. But though this tragic story provides some Native American context to where we're floating and hiking and camping, only a few episodes actually took place along the Salmon, and so we don't feel the connection very directly. On our river journey, there aren't any battlefields to visit, and little or no evidence remains of the war or the people—any Indian people, recent or prehistoric.

Along the river, we are left only with a few well-concealed

pictographs and petroglyphs, or the occasional arrowhead—rare indications that the western wilderness was something other, and far older, than simply *our* frontier. But that's a lesson worth learning as we reconsider the myth of the American West and strive to make it more inclusive so that it can continue to serve its many purposes—among them, helping to keep our dreams of possibility alive.

The Shorts Bar pictographs are some of the best on the Salmon; they consist of primitive red drawings of what appear to be suns and arrows, human and dream figures, geometric shapes and swirls that might represent God or Death or the River, depending upon your interpretation. They are painted with care on an undercut rock face that would have made for a cozy shelter. In fact, there's some indication that a few pit houses were constructed at the base of the rock.

Some say the pictographs were religious in nature, the painting of them a ritual in itself. Others opine that they were purely decorative. However you interpret these bright splashes on the dark basalt walls, they are beautiful and eerie. Ghostly postcards sent by expressive hands from another era, saying: the weather is fine, wish we were here.

The No-More-Salmon River

"The rivers are our brothers. They quench our thirst. The rivers carry our canoes and feed our children. You must give the rivers the kindness you would give your brothers."
CHIEF SEATTLE OF THE DUWAMISH TRIBE

"Love of wilderness is an expression of loyalty to the earth, the earth which bore us and sustains us, the only home we will ever know, the only paradise we ever need—if only we had the eyes to see it."
EDWARD ABBEY, *DESERT SOLITAIRE*

"Many Americans came to understand that wilderness was essential for pioneering: without wild country the concepts of frontier and pioneer were meaningless. The villain, it appeared, was as vital to the play as the hero, and, in view of the admirable qualities that contact with wilderness were thought to have produced, perhaps not as villainous as supposed. Toward the end of the nineteenth century, esteem for the frontiersman extended to include his environment. Pioneering, in short, came to be regarded as important not only for spearheading the advance of civilization, but also for bringing Americans into contact with the primitive."
RODERICK NASH, *WILDERNESS AND THE AMERICAN MIND*

While we are floating downstream through a tranquil flatwater section of the river on our way toward Warren Creek Camp on a hot, lazy August afternoon, one of my passengers—a fly-fisherman named Bob, from Connecticut—asks me if he has any chance of actually catching a salmon in the Salmon River.

Holding my oars steady with my palms, blades poised above the water, I let the boat drift, and tell him that sure he has a chance. I consider adding that he probably has a better chance of hooking a winning Lotto ticket. Or a mermaid. But instead I say, "If you're after Sockeye, I think about three of them made it back upstream from the ocean this year."

For salmon the fish, Salmon the River has truly become a river of no return.

Like many guides, I've already grown weary of lecturing guests about the importance of not only loving the outdoors, but also of fighting to protect what little wilderness remains in this country—whether by writing letters, recycling, donating to environmental organizations, voting green, or chaining themselves to bulldozers. Though most of us who work out here feel pain, anger, outrage, frustration, and sadness that even such a sacred and supposedly protected place as the Salmon River still faces constant, vicious, senseless, and unnecessary degradation, we often strive to hold our emotions in check. We know that lecturing people who are on vacation may cause them to tune us out, and that we need to get through to folks in other, more subtle ways.

So I don't tell Bob that maybe we should rename this waterway "The No-More-Salmon River," or "The We-Killed-All-The-Salmon River." I keep my mouth shut for a change, hoping that his disappointment might ferment into outrage—and, eventually, action—on its own.

At least until the last century, salmon began and ended their spirited and adventuresome lives in cold, clear western rivers and streams—as they'd done for about five million years. They constituted the very soul of the Pacific Northwest. Over the millennia, when salmon migrated from inland waterways they carried biological materials from the continent out to sea. Upon returning to their birth streams to spawn a few years later, they transported materials from the ocean back up into the heart of the continent, into mountains thousands of feet high and hundreds of miles from the Pacific. Salmon provided a genetic link between these vastly different but equally essential and ultimately interconnected ecosystems. They coursed through the arteries and veins of the region, always returning to the heart.

Salmon also sustained—physically and spiritually—Native American tribes throughout the Northwest. Early white explorers described the rivers as being so thick with salmon that you could practically walk across the water on the backs of the fish. They stood as a symbol of the bounty of western wilderness.

Today, the government lists three species of Salmon River salmon—Sockeye, Fall Chinook and Spring/Summer Chinook—as endangered, and several other subspecies have already gone extinct. You cannot separate salmon from the Salmon River; assaults on one threaten the other. The fact that compared to a century ago hardly any salmon currently return to spawn in the river suggests that something is seriously amiss in the western landscape. And since we depend on the land and waters not just to foster the uplifting power of myth, but for our very lives, we are in danger, too.

Talking about recent and ongoing threats to salmon populations throughout the West, Ric Bailey, O.A.R.S.-Dories guide and Executive Director of the Hells Canyon Preservation Council, says, "Salmon used to define every culture that ever existed in the Columbia Basin. There is no excuse for allowing any activity that could potentially further degrade salmon habitat. When we talk about losing these fish, we're talking about losing the biological foundation of the entire Pacific Northwest. Everything in this ecosystem revolves around salmon, going back beyond even the aboriginal cultures."

It's ironic that in the course of "conquering" the wilderness, pioneers destroyed the very thing that both made their pioneering possible and supposedly fashioned them into the kind of people they were: the wide expanse of untamed lands that seemed to stretch limitlessly across America. Turnerism and the western myth celebrated our subduing of nature throughout this vast territory. But Turner at least recognized that the frontier was not only finite; he claimed that we'd already pursued it to its very limits by the end of the nineteenth century. In contrast, the western myth continues to celebrate the triumph of man over nature without recognizing that if taming wilderness made us a great people, then the relentless civilizing of wild lands necessarily means that at some fast-approaching time we'll have to become a different people, because we will have already tamed our last bit of wilderness.

Many people take wilderness trips in places like the Salmon River because they want to experience the frontier nature of backcountry and see how it effects them. They wish to feel something of the pioneer spirit that made our nation great. But in spite of its legal protections, even the Salmon—the last major free-flowing river in the Lower 48—is under siege from interests (including our own government) that still pursue a long-outdated remnant of the western myth to its furthest extreme: the idea that developing and exploiting natural resources is the only sensible way of using them—a view as limited as believing that you can explain all of western American history by describing the experiences of cocky white males.

Throughout the West right now, industrial entities who've historically reaped profits by exploiting the land have banded together politically to fight environmentalists. These groups go by many names and rally around slogans that sound reasonable and sympathetic: The Wise Use Movement, Oregon Citizens Alliance, The Contract With America.

While there's always another side to every story, and while plenty of moral, hard-working, environmentally-concerned farmers and ranchers and loggers have every right to pursue their livelihoods responsibly in appropriate places, in this story the side of the corporate land users is simply dead wrong. Don't ever trust these industry-backed faux-populists—not for a moment, not a word they say. Their continued support of activities that pollute and degrade the earth on a large scale, particularly on public lands, suggests that they are far worse than simply shortsighted; their actions and views suggest that they are so deeply irresponsible as just not to care about anything besides economic values. They'd apparently sell out our heritage and rob their own children of the chance to experience wilderness and spend time along the kind of geographical frontier that has done so much for us as individuals, and as a nation. And at the same time that they're destroying what's left of the frontier and all it represents, at the same time they're robbing the planet that so graciously supports us, they call themselves patriots, and wave the flag in your face.

Rage against these heartless, foolish industry flunkies and their deceptions and rhetoric. Do not believe that it's still okay to fell the last five percent of our old-growth forests, leave toxic mine tailings piled on the land, build roads into wilderness, and "inadvertently" kill salmon in the course of enriching their bank accounts. Because what they haven't mentioned—and perhaps haven't even figured out for themselves—is that those salmon offer us a glimpse into our own future; those salmon are swimming out in front of us, in the same direction that we're headed on our way downstream.

Today, irresponsible logging, livestock grazing, jet boating, and hydro power construction and operation present the most serious environmental threats to salmon (or what's left of them)—that powerful symbol of Northwest wilderness—and to the Salmon River. Even though I've given up on outright lecturing, few of my passengers complete their river journeys without my schooling them in at least the basic facts about how these activities destroy some of what little remains of our wild western frontier.

For starters, even logging taking place miles away can effect the balance of ecosystems such as the one that has evolved over millions of years along the Salmon River. When loggers cut trees in a mountain watershed—particularly in places like the Salmon River country, where the slopes are steep and the soil is highly erodible—they remove the anchors that hold the soil in place. When it rains on a logged hillside, runoff can cause landslides in which tons of soil and sediment pile into the river. This not only devastates the ecology of the former forest by washing away soil that might have again supported life; the sediment also ravages the river. Sediment ruins the spawning grounds of salmon by covering over and suffocating millions of eggs that the fish have laid in the previously clean gravel of the river bottom, and by permanently destroying the river bed for future generations of egg-laying fish, until there are no more fish.

When we float past Mallard Creek, sometimes I casually mention that ten miles up the creek, the Forest Service recently sold a large block of ancient cedar and pines to a timber company for clear-cutting. Logging also occurs on private land along the Lower Salmon, and other timber activity is being planned between Vinegar Creek and Riggins. In fact, the Forest Service and the BLM actually manage our National Forests in the interest of timber companies. These government agencies spend more money building roads into the woods, so that corporations like Weyerhaeuser and Louisiana Pacific can log the forests, than they charge these companies for the trees.

In *River of No Return*, Carrey and Conley describe the Forest Service's plan, back in the seventies, to sell a cut of 28,000,000 board feet of timber annually, on 59,000 previously roadless acres of remote Salmon River country. This description still pretty well characterizes the government's role in liquidating public forests at a loss. "The trees will be expensive to harvest, but since the timber buyer receives full costs for removal plus thirteen per cent for profit and risk, taxpayers will subsidize the logging. If one happened to be both taxpayer and fisherman, it might make him mad enough to raise hell and put a chunk under it."

Although some folks take comfort in the cushy country image of cows grazing along the slopes beside the more developed sections of the Salmon that we run, I occasionally point out that the cow pies littering the banks and beaches should provide enough argument against cupping their hands for a cool, refreshing drink.

Even within the Wild and Scenic corridor, cows rule, although we don't often see them here while we're on river trips because during the summer they head for cooler pastures at higher elevations. Just as the cows themselves are sometimes difficult to find, some of their impacts are also hard to discern. But they're as real as a thousand-pound Black Angus standing on your toe.

Most guests on a river trip have no conception of what the Salmon River corridor is supposed to look like in its natural state, so they can't know that what appears in some places to be perfectly normal vegetation actually consists of a melange of cheat grass, star thistle, napweed, and other noxious invader species that have virtually mugged local species, such as bunch grass. Bunch grass once grew prolifically along the river in four-foot high clumps that provided cover for sharp-tailed grouse. Now, however, no sharp-tailed grouse remain because cows ate all their cover and the grouse became the equivalent of fast food for hawks and other predators. When the cows finished off the last of the bunch grass, invader species moved in and established a cozy niche.

Cattle also impact other river wildlife, at least indirectly, because wherever they graze, ranchers and government agencies institute large-scale predator control programs—a prettied-up way of saying that they shoot, trap, and poison such indigenous species as coyotes, wolves, cougars, eagles, and bears. When folks are surprised that they don't encounter more wildlife along the Salmon, I sometimes tell them that cows killed off most of the other animals.

But the biggest impact of cattle along the Salmon River is on the water quality of the river itself and so, necessarily, on fish. Cattle pollute the river both directly, by defecating in and around it, and by facilitating erosion of the river banks. When the water rises during spring runoff, all that soil and crap washes into the river and settles on the spawning beds, suffocating salmon eggs and permanently ruining the beds the same way that erosion from logged hillsides does. Just like with timber sales, the Forest Service and the BLM lose money by leasing grazing rights on public lands along the river for approximately twenty percent of what they would cost on private land.

I'm happy to report that most of our guests are shocked when the first jet boat roars past them on the water—and even more so when they learn that the government allows so many jet boats on a river it has officially designated as "Wild and Scenic." A guide usually explains to the group that legislators grandfathered this use of wilderness into law on behalf of constituents who owned fishing lodges along the river and had historically accessed them by jet boat over the previous decades. But it's also clear that commercial outfitters have made a joke of this loophole by running a profusion of day-trips up and down the river.

For some people, I guess the tourist brochures make this sound like the perfect trip, the grandest adventure: riding a sleek, speeding silver jet boat through dangerous rapids while gripping the safety railing and screaming with glee. And still making it back to your motel by dinner time. But this, as much as anything, constitutes a wild frontier experience drained of any wildness, or any of the rewards implicit in confronting the frontier.

As Leon says about jet boats, "The philosophy of anybody who would take you down a river with motors is different. They probably have more limited values. On a motorized trip, you're like a smoker in a room full of nonsmokers, especially on a road-less, pristine river where people come seeking peace and beauty and quiet. Motorized trips just don't follow natural rhythms."

While there's certainly a place for this type of recreation, that place isn't along a wild and scenic river corridor where other folks have come to experience the backcountry. Jet boats have plenty of room to tour passengers along the roaded and developed sections of the Salmon.

Ric Bailey spends most of his off-river time fighting jet boat use on the Snake and Salmon Rivers. In response to his efforts, he's received death threats and has been hung in effigy in his home town. Nobody is more articulate and passionate when speaking about the threats jet boats pose to the wilderness character of wild rivers.

Bailey says, "The environmental impacts of jet boats are very real, but the primary problem is the social consequences. Jet boats are turning the Salmon and Snake Rivers into motorized zip-in, zip-out tourist traps. Where once you used to experience the river on its own terms by flowing with the water and camping on the beaches, now you can take a jet boat with fifty other people, at fifty miles an hour, straight up the gut of the river in one day.

"Jet boats belittle the rapids; the pressure waves and wakes they create disturb salmon and erode the beaches; and they're turning the canyons into noise chambers reverberating from 900-horsepower engines and exhaust systems. When you get off a jet boat your memory of the Salmon River will be of eagles fleeing, of a metallic vibration roaring through your head, of smashing through rapids. I've seen float trip passengers whose experience was ruined because, in their opinion, with the number of jet boats on the river, they might as well have gone camping on the Santa Anna Freeway."

Jet boaters take to the river with that same conqueror's attitude, that same celebration of man over nature that's "civilized" so much of the West. Which is to say they've robbed the place of an essential component of its wild character.

As Ric Bailey concludes, "The jet boat issue is about allowing the Salmon River to maintain the dignity of owning itself instead of being owned. Jet boaters essentially confront and defy the river. Upstream traffic, especially, defies its dignity. It's contrary to the nature of the way things flow."

But jet boats can also perform a vital function along the river: since our passengers are guaranteed to encounter this environmental abuse directly—whereas they might not actually see cows grazing or loggers felling trees or the dams that have devastated salmon populations—and they're not likely to enjoy the encounter, jet boats may just make them mad enough to take some action.

To appreciate the significance of the fact that the Salmon River remains undammed, it's important for guests to understand a little bit more about these structures—more than 50,000 of which, according to Marc Reisner, author of *Cadillac Desert,* hold this nation's rivers hostage. Though none span the Salmon River itself, plenty of dams downstream on the Snake and Columbia Rivers have managed to wreak horrible impacts on fish that would have spawned in the Salmon if they could have gotten there. Following that same notion of the western myth that suggests that subduing nature is our challenge and duty—our Manifest Destiny—the Bureau of Reclamation, the Army Corps of Engineers, and other private and governmental agencies undertook a frenzy of dam building earlier in this century without adequately predicting and compensating for the immense impacts their actions would have on the environment.

In terms of salmon and other migratory fish, dams are like cholesterol blocking the arteries that the fish swim along. When salmon swimming upstream from the ocean to spawn encounter a concrete dam several hundred feet high, they cannot get back home, and they die without spawning. After this happens a few years consecutively, all the old salmon will have died, and no new generation will have been born to replace them. A single dam can wipe out entire genetic stocks of fish, which have developed through complex evolutionary processes over millions of years. Although engineers have designed a number of ways to help fish around dams, none have worked particularly well.

Biologists once thought the biggest problem was that dams prevented fish from migrating upstream. But juvenile fish cannot get downstream past the dams, either. Although most dams contain diversion systems, many fish end up missing the diversions and getting killed in the hydropower turbines.

Furthermore, salmon are driven downstream by an instinct that compels them to follow the flow of the river out to sea. But dams create giant reservoirs that may stretch for a hundred miles, and which contain virtually no discernible flow. When fish gliding downstream on the current encounter these pools of flat water, they can't tell which way is downstream any more. They may swim around in circles until the increased water temperature of the reservoirs kills them, or they're picked off by predators.

Engineers have devised other systems also meant to save fish by counteracting the devastating effects of dams, but if any of these had worked, salmon might still thrive in the Salmon River. In the past decade, the government has grown so desperate to improve hugely declining fish runs—mostly because of economic considerations—that they began transporting fish around the dams on barges, and driving fish upstream in the backs of trucks, like hitchhikers they were kind enough to stop for along the road. Not surprisingly, neither of these methods worked very well, either.

For a time, scientists believed that raising fish in hatcheries and then releasing large numbers into rivers might bolster the declining runs. But the additional problems created by hatcheries provide further evidence of just how complex natural systems are. Particular species of salmon have spent millennia adapting to very specific characteristics of the particular streams they inhabit—such as water temperatures, vegetation and gravel types, the amount of shade along the banks, and the types, active seasons, and numbers of predators. Expecting them to thrive when you pull fish out of some river, raise a few million of their eggs, and release the young fish into an entirely different stream would be like dropping humans on Jupiter and expecting us to start breathing methane. Most high school biology students would recognize this most basic concept of evolution.

In addition, hatchery fish are notoriously weak, sickly, and dispirited. When hatchery biologists release large numbers of these fish into a stream, they mate with wild fish and dilute the gene pool; in effect, they counteract natural selection and create piscine versions of the kinds of mutants who chased Burt Reynolds and John Voight in the movie *Deliverance*.

All of which is a way of saying that although no dams interrupt the flow of the Salmon River, dams downstream have interrupted the life cycle of fish that would have populated the Salmon—as they always had —if dams hadn't cut them off from their homes. And since river systems are interdependent, you can't construct a dam on one river and expect to limit the adverse consequences to that single waterway.

When a person can't catch a salmon in the Salmon River, it represents far more than a disappointing moment on vacation; it's far worse than just sad. It is a symbol for everything that's wrong with our environment, and there'll be plenty more such symbols to come if we destroy our remaining wilderness frontiers. A century after Frederick Jackson Turner mistakenly announced that the frontier—that very thing which made us Americans, and good—had closed, now we are really in danger of closing what remains of it by destroying the little wild land that still survives.

As Ric Bailey says, "If we're willing to sacrifice the most critical component of this place that we call home in order to have cheaper electricity, in order to continue logging irresponsibly so we can have cheaper lumber; if we can't make those small kinds of sacrifices, we're in deep trouble as a species. If we can't save salmon, then we can't save ourselves."

Saving ourselves involves letting go of an attitude—now a component of the western myth—that worked for us as American pioneers two hundred years ago, but is leading us toward the brink of disaster today: the notion that we are separate from our environment and that we can continue to exploit our wild lands as if they might stretch infinitely westward toward the setting sun.

The Slide

"In the very last analysis, none of us knows whether this is wholly a secular world. But if there are Spirits, surely they must reside in the mountain West. Their special places, where they most prefer to dip and twirl and revel must be in the deep canyons. Of those places, they must savor most of all those mystical spots where the power is the greatest, where the big canyons form narrow corridors and the rivers gather up all of their strength and rush and foam and rage in order to push through."
CHARLES WILKINSON, *THE EAGLE BIRD*

"I still get tense. I have long conversations with myself: 'Why don't you stay back in town and settle for something more civilized, because now you've got five overweight people and you've got to get down the river, and if they fall in they're probably going to die on you?' It's scary trying to talk yourself into taking the risks."
KURT WALD, RIVER GUIDE, ON RUNNING BIG WATER

"I don't know if any of them ever felt that much adrenaline before. When you have that much adrenaline going through your body it's like you're living a whole 'nother life for a short period of time. They were thrilled with being there and performing through that."
LONNIE HUTSON, RIVER GUIDE, DESCRIBING TAKING DORY PASSENGERS THROUGH THE SLIDE AT 29,000 CFS

Four other guides and I are standing on a granite boulder—part of an enormous rock slide—in the narrowest part of Blue Canyon, on the Lower Salmon. We're scouting a rapid called "The Slide," named after the geologic feature we're perched on. The rapid appears as a mess of rocks, waves, and holes stretching across the current in a tight archipelago, making passage an intricate dance. Below The Slide the afternoon will turn golden as we float mostly calm water to where the Salmon converges with the Snake River, and beyond that to our takeout at Heller Bar. Then we'll load up our gear and drive fast back toward Lewiston, to hot showers, clean clothes, and cocktails and a trip dinner in the back room at Jonathan's.

At low water The Slide is hardly even a rapid, but as the river rises, more and more water must funnel through this narrow, bending constriction in the canyon, creating giant waves that boil up and curl sideways off the steep walls. My map and guide to the Lower Salmon River includes a special warning which says that The Slide "ranges from barely a riffle at flows under 10,000 cfs, to Class V–VI at flows of 20,000 and higher. In very high water these are the most dangerous rapids on the Lower Salmon River and unrunnable. These rapids cannot be lined or portaged without great difficulty. Scouting is mandatory and quite hard." Today the river is running at 28,000 cfs, and my pulse isn't far behind.

At the entrance to The Slide, a tongue of green water constricts in a narrow vee directly into the heart of the rapid. The real muscle consists of one humongous wave in the very center of the river that surges and breaks irregularly, so you can't possibly predict how it might act when you row into it. This wall of water crests high, crashes down like an ocean wave, swells, and collapses off to the sides. To the right of it, the river drops over a series of ledges and boulders, creating deep recirculating holes—Maytag holes. Just to the left, a lateral wave pushes off from shore right into the main wave. And just downstream of this gauntlet, directly below the biggest wave, a second huge lateral curls off the right wall. The real challenge in running The Slide is finding a way to hit the main wave and the lateral below it—one facing directly upstream, the other coming in from the side at a ninety-degree angle—head on so that they can't flip you over sideways. Guiding a boat through this confusing maelstrom is like sprinting across a short stretch of open ground under sniper fire.

Joel, who has run The Slide many more times than the rest of us combined, is visibly nervous while scouting the rapid, which makes me nervous, too. He stares at the water and ghost rows it—practicing the moves he'll make on his oars, where he'll pull hard, where he'll pivot. Joel has an eighty-year old man in his boat who'll face a very tough swim if anything goes wrong. As Joel ghosts the run with deep concentration, Brannon skillfully mimics Joel's actions. He, too, jauntily pulls on imaginary oars, then he genuflects, scratches his balls, rubs one hand up his other arm giving the sign to steal second base. I can't help laughing, although there's nothing funny about where we are. I wonder if Brannon is nervous, and just can't tell.

Leon, with whom I've been through plenty of adventures backpacking and canyoneering and rock climbing in Utah, and who never seems afraid, is *really* nervous, since he's the trip leader and ultimately responsible for any mishaps. He also has a six-year old boy as a passenger. His nervousness unsettles me even more.

Trista, a trainee on her first whitewater trip ever at this early point in the season, and my only passenger, isn't nervous at all, which scares the bjeezus out of me. This is also my first time on this particular stretch of river—I'm running a gear boat to earn my license on this section—so I have no previous experience in

The Slide to draw on.

As we study every intricate detail of the rapid, every clue to running it safely, I feel a strong need to pee, which isn't unusual when I'm scouting difficult water. Although rapids are rated on a scale of Class I to Class VI based on their potential for upset and injury, another scale might as easily convey the danger to our passengers: how many of their boatmen stop to relieve themselves while examining the rapid from shore.

We stand on the balanced rock and admire—and fear—the river's power, and visualize our individual journeys through the rapid. We listen to the roar of whitewater reverberating through the canyon. I focus on a rock jutting up to the surface just off the left shore, visible only occasionally as a wave breaks and surges over it—part of the river's subconscious, what makes it behave the way it does. This rock will serve as one of my key markers in finding my way through the run. Whitewater always looks different when you're actually on it, so it's good to use the terrain as a sort of route map.

When we've discussed—ten or twelve times—every possible way of running The Slide, and I've asked questions that the more experienced boatmen can't possibly answer—what happens if you hit the first wave head on? Is the lateral below it big enough to flip a gear raft?—Joel, showing signs of wear, says he's ready. We nod, volunteering to watch him, to see if that gives us any additional information. As Joel disappears around the rock slide back up toward his boat, I glance downriver, where below the rapid Curt Chang waits in a jet boat as a safety precaution.

It's the first time I've ever even heard of such a thing.

Part of me truly hates this, and says let's flip and swim and swallow water if that's how it goes, because that's what we're here for. That part of me says we don't need no steen-king jet boat, and that if I screw up and the jet boat motors over to rescue me, maybe I'll pull a Martin Litton and refuse to climb on.

On the other hand, part of me is truly grateful to see Curt standing by. Later in the summer I learned that on Curt's own first descent of The Slide, his group flipped five of six dories. So he's probably happy to be offering some backup, too.

Tension over running The Slide actually started building yesterday morning, when we woke up planning to run it that afternoon. We knew the water was still high but had been dropping steadily every day. Nobody seemed especially nervous, although no one was talking about it, either.

We ate breakfast early in case scouting should take us a long time. As we were finishing our French toast and bacon and sipping a last cup of coffee and waiting for the sun to warm the beach before we started breaking camp, we heard the droning of a small aircraft overhead. After passing right above us once, the plane circled back at an altitude of about fifty feet and the pilot tossed something out the window which landed right in the middle of camp.

I'd already been looking for signs on this trip that might in some way foreshadow our experience at The Slide. Last night, a passenger had discovered a small rattlesnake not far from the open door of her tent. This morning we watched a buck swim across the river toward us, then turn and head back for the other shore, scampering up just before the current washed him into a small rapid. While these events were open to interpretation, in terms of signs neither could compare to an actual message dropped into our midst from an airplane.

When Leon retrieved the cylinder the pilot had tossed out to us, a note inside read: "Slide still high. Recommend waiting another day as water drops. Will provide jet boat support if wanted. Please signal if you want jet boat this afternoon at 2:30." The note was from Curt Chang.

At first I thought it was some kind of joke, but then it brought home for the first time the true nature of where we were; in spite of the jet boats and air strips and the cows grazing beside the river, in spite of the long roaded section we'd come through, and all the other floaters we'd seen, we were traveling through an inaccessible wilderness. The only way a message could've reached us was if someone dropped it out of an airplane after first discerning where we were camped. And the only way out of the canyon right now was downriver, through The Slide. This was our frontier, both internal and external, both real and mythical.

After taking a few moments to think about our options, Leon decided we should wait until tomorrow and run the rapid with jet boat support. We spelled out the word "no" with orange lifejackets, in response to whether we wanted the jet boat that afternoon, and Leon planned to radio a message to Curt later, telling him what time we'd run The Slide tomorrow morning. However, after the airplane departed, we discovered that our radio wasn't working. We managed to flag down a couple of river rangers motoring past camp, and asked if they could relay the message that Curt should send support at eleven A.M. the following day. We had no idea whether Curt would get the message, and even less of an idea what The Slide would really be like if Curt had gone to all that trouble and expense just to have us wait one more day.

Since we were already only about eight miles from the entrance to Blue Canyon—and once you entered the canyon there was no place to camp upstream of The Slide—we decided to spend a leisurely morning. We played horseshoes, fired up another pot of coffee, and took our time breaking camp. In the late morning we set out to make the few miles to the last camp above Blue Canyon.

But an hour later, as we searched for that camp, we only passed rocky beaches and gravel bars with no place to park our boats. None of us had ever seen the river at this water level, so where Joel had thought there might be a nice sandy stretch at lower water, today that spot could easily lie under six or eight feet of river. In the distance, where the Salmon took a couple of broad turns, we glimpsed a narrow, bare, exposed strip of sand, but we had already stopped in a small eddy on the opposite shore. The current was rushing downstream so quickly we weren't certain we'd be able to ferry across, and if we missed this beach, the river would sweep us around the corner into Blue Canyon, and we'd either have to run The Slide or make camp on our boats, tied up to boulders.

We had a tough pull to catch the eddy below the beach, and we all just barely made it. My arms went numb from the exertion, but I was happy to be there, although the temperature was well over 100 degrees. We set up a shade tarp right away—which the hot wind blew down three or four times—and many of our guests climbed up to a basalt ledge under the scant shade of a couple of hackberry trees and tried to get comfortable. A few others set their chairs right in the river, and sat half in the water drinking lemonade, creating what we liked to call "the hippo bar."

By evening, the sky grew dark and menacing with storm clouds, heightening the sense of dread I felt about The Slide. But since it was our last night out, Brannon and I mixed up a Mr. Bucket punch—consisting of orange soda, cranberry and orange juices, rum, vodka, bananas, canned pineapples, giant chunks of ice, and anything else we discovered in coolers and hatches that seemed like it might work. The two of us cooked dinner in a warm, humid, comforting buzz and our guests gathered around the punch and under the shade tarp as the air cooled and a few scattered raindrops fell.

Just as we finished our chicken teriyaki the skies opened up. We arranged chairs around the fire pan under the tarp and sat watching one of the most violent and beautiful thunderstorms I have ever seen. Joel broke out his Hasselblad—a tall camera case that makes the perfect waterproof holder for a bottle of Bushmill's whiskey, a bottle of brandy, and various accouterments. I sipped Bushmill's from my Dories mug, feeling myself warm again from the inside out, and watched the storm rage above the dark walls that marked the entrance to Blue Canyon. We watched the moon rise, luminescent, between clouds and brown peaks and patches of cobalt sky. Lightning forked in long, jagged bursts, and rain pounded down. We sat in silence. There was no need to speak. We were warm and dry and still safe, and there wasn't much reason to think about tomorrow.

Some time later the rain stopped and we moved our chairs beneath the open sky and built a larger fire. We made S'mores—sandwiches of fire-roasted marshmallows and chocolate wedged between graham crackers. Leon gave a reading, and we went around the circle offering our favorite moments from the trip. We'd been through some things together, some of us, and tight bonds had formed. The guides presented an award to Stew, who was our first commercial passenger ever to travel the Middle Fork, Main, and Lower Salmon Rivers on a single seventeen-day trip. Brannon escorted him down to the dory named the Glen Canyon, and had Stew sign his name on the inside of the front hatch. An inevitable sadness hung over us; regardless of what happened at The Slide tomorrow, this party would be breaking up.

I slept fitfully that night. Rain pattered on my tent intermittently, and I kept sliding down the sloping beach. My back hurt and my fingers felt numb from rowing, and I really just didn't want to run The Slide. I hoped that something would prevent it: perhaps the river rangers would forbid us and insist on hauling us back upstream by jet boat to the take-out at Eagle Creek.

I also *wanted* to run The Slide, right then. I knew I verged on the edge of my own frontier, and I was anxious to pass through to the wilder side of it; having to wait until morning was pure agony. This was exactly what river trips could do for any of us who ventured out on them: take us up to some perceived limit, and offer us the chance to grow slightly larger, to range outside the fence of comfort that usually keeps us waiting passively in the corral.

That night I actually dreamed about the rapid, seeing it almost exactly as it would look in the morning, although nobody had ever described it to me. I saw the run that Joel would first advise against, and then eventually recommend.

Breakfast conversations were hushed, and the guides attended to rigging our boats with uncharacteristic solemnity. I found everything irritating—the dirt on my cooler lid, the way somebody spoke to me—which was how I recognized just how nervous I must be. I tried to take slow, deep breaths.

After what seemed an interminable morning of breaking camp and "rigging for a flip"—making certain that every last item was cinched down so that if the boat went over we wouldn't lose any gear—we were off. A mile or so into the tight confines of Blue Canyon, in the chilly air beneath an overcast sky, we saw the landslide on the left shore that marked the rapid. We pulled into a tight, tiny eddy and tied up the boats with great foreboding.

As we climbed around on the boulders to get a look, we could hear The Slide, see the horizon line of the river and the mist kicking high above it.

Standing on the rocks in the high roar of the rapid, we wait for Joel's dory to come around the corner. When it appears, he's standing in his footwell with his hands on the oars, looking a little like Henry Fonda in *On Golden Pond*. As the slow water above the rapid carries him toward the green tongue, he sits back and works the oars to set his position. Then the current grabs his boat and tugs him in. He hits the big wave exactly where he said he would, just to the left of its crest. His dory tilts upward until it's nearly vertical, perches on top, kicks, and slides down the other side—a clean, perfect entry.

The moment he's cleared the apex, Joel pivots away from the second lateral wave coming in from the right just below the big wave. The lateral crashes down on the stern and side of the boat, pushing the other side way up in the air and threatening to flip it. Tom, who's riding up front, leans his entire weight far out over the high side of the boat and keeps it from going over. Then just as it looks as if they've cleared all the danger, and Joel's passengers begin bailing and raising their arms in victory, the momentum of the lateral wave transfers to the dory and sends it shooting across the current and smashes it into the left wall—wham! When the boat hits they rock forward like crash test dummies and I think they might actually fly from the craft, or get whiplash. Finally, the boat disappears around a corner and then reappears in an eddy a quarter mile downstream, and it looks like everyone is okay.

After watching Joel's run, Leon takes a long, long time scouting—at least another forty-five minutes. I grow more and more irritable because every moment that we wait, the fear notches up just a little higher in my chest until I can barely swallow. After Leon finally starts upstream toward his dory, he stops on another rock and watches the river some more.

A couple of minutes later we can see Leon rowing out toward the center of the river. He catches the green tongue that feeds right into the giant center wave, but where Joel pulled a bit to the left, Leon hits it straight on. The boat rises and twists, knocking Leon out of his seat. As one side comes up, Leon—lying spread-eagled on the deck—tries to grab onto something to keep from sliding over the side. Then the dory hits the second wave sideways and it rights the boat and then pitches the opposite side in the air. Hitting the second wave is the only thing that keeps Leon from tumbling out. When they've cleared the second wave Leon scrambles back to his oars and pulls the boat away from the wall and safely downstream.

Brannon runs right after Leon, in his raft, with Corinne as his one passenger up front. He picks a line much farther to the left, and catches the giant first wave on the side. Corinne takes most of the wave over the top of her. The boat spins left, toward the wall, but with weak momentum. Brannon loses an oar for a moment, then retrieves it, pulls into the main current, and sails on.

I stand up on the rocks watching all of this and shaking my head. I'm waiting for that moment when I'll know I've seen enough to feel confident, but I also know that moment won't come. I scout for another ten minutes, finally making a decision that I feel is necessary, but which I am totally unsure of, and there's nobody left to ask. I think I see a better line through the rapid than anyone else has taken—pulling backwards and letting an eddy along the right shore help set me up.

The others are safe now, even if their runs haven't been stellar, and that puts even more pressure on me. To screw up now means being alone in it, means not living up to the standards set by my fellow guides and implied by the powerful western myth. This undercurrent defines my entire summer, though I'm not fully aware of it at this time.

It is also a moment of pure independence and individualism: to decide upon a different run than any of the other boatmen saw or attempted is a frightening prospect. I am alone in the world for these few moments; nobody can help me and I have no choice but just to GO. And a mistake here means a flip or a bad swim at the very least.

When I've finally seen enough, I walk back toward my boat, stopping to glance at the river as the perspective changes, trying to memorize landmarks that will tell me where I am when I'm on the water and the rapid looks different. I listen to the melody and bass of the river, which contains all voices, all sounds. Sometimes it floats one up to the surface: the voice of my father; the music from a time in my life I'll never know again—things left behind.

It's strange to be up here by myself. Trista has already begun walking back to the boat; she seems bored, preoccupied, bothered a little by all the fuss.

As I untie the raft I'm clearly mumbling to myself. I ask her if she absolutely understands what high-siding means. I rehearse my run one last time, reminding myself to strive for a Zen-like balance between power and finesse.

As I float into the tongue, I pivot my boat perpendicular to the current, stern to the left shore, and look for my marker rock. The moment I see that momentum has just about carried me past it, I pull backwards hard in that direction with short, crisp strokes. I punch the small lateral coming off that wall with my stern and it stops my momentum dead and gently nudges me back toward the big wave, but at the same time the downstream current drops me just below it. The big wave crashes on the side of my boat. I pull hard on my right oar to swing the bow around to hit the second lateral wave—the one that propelled Joel into the wall—head on and forward. It tumbles down on us in a world of white and for a moment I can't see anything. I lose all perspective and have plenty of time in which to wonder if we might flip. The wave grabs one of my oars and I let go rather than letting the power of the water propel me right out of the boat.

A moment later the world clears and I grab the loose oar and row shakily into the main current. I scream as loud as I can—a whoop not so much of victory as release, draining the tension that has built up in me, releasing it into the cool, wet air.

It's over that fast—like gunfire, or bungi jumping, or sex; plenty of buildup, and then boom: closure, and I feel myself disconnect, and then I can't even recall how it all happened. I can barely pull into the eddy below the rapid because my legs are shaking so and my muscles seem to have gone dead.

It was not—after all that—a big deal. And yet it was. We were all just a little different after running The Slide—both as a group and as individuals. It was a defining moment, yet one I have difficulty explaining, as if it changed something in me at a level where I couldn't quite see it clearly, but simply knew it to be true. I'd crossed a threshold—a frontier line, Frederick Jackson Turner might have said in a lighter moment, if he had lighter moments.

I had the opportunity to run The Slide again, in late August, at 7000 cfs—a quarter of its earlier flow. Since I'd earned my license on that first trip, I now carried two passengers, and as we entered Blue Canyon I told them the story about the airplane and the message. I told them that a week after our run, another dory flipped in the rapid. I tried to describe the monstrous waves, and how scared I was.

When we came around the corner where the rock slide angles down from the left shore, we could see the rapid: a couple of tiny waves not even large enough to sport whitecaps on top. My passengers looked at me with a hint of amusement and a generous dose of disbelief.

Boatmen have become the docents of oral tradition on the river—not only keeping alive the old pioneering stories, but promulgating an oral history of our own. The story of The Slide had already entered the realm of minor myth by then, but I knew that even though I described things just as they happened, my passengers were asking themselves that age-old boatmen's riddle:

How do you know when a river guide is lying?

The answer: his lips are moving.

Take-out

"Do not burn yourselves out, be as I am—a reluctant enthusiast...a part-time crusader, a half-hearted fanatic. Save the other half of yourselves and your lives for pleasure and adventure. It is not enough to fight for the West: it is even more important to enjoy it. While you can. While it's still here. So get out there and hunt and fish and mess around with your friends, ramble out yonder and explore the forests, encounter the grizz, climb the mountains, bag the peaks, run the rivers, breathe deep of that yet sweet and lucid air, sit quietly for a while and contemplate the precious stillness, that lovely, mysterious, and awesome space. Enjoy yourselves, keep your brain in your head and your head firmly attached to your body, the body active and live, and I promise you this much; I promise you this one sweet victory over our enemies, over those desk bound men with their hearts in a safe deposit box and their eyes hypnotized by desk calculators. I promise you this: you will outlive the bastards."
EDWARD ABBEY

Shall we gather at the river
Where bright angel feet have trod;
With its crystal tide forever
Flowing by the throne of God?

Shall we gather at the river
The beautiful, the beautiful river;
Gather with the saints at the river,
That flows by the throne of the Lord?
ROBERT LOWRY, 1864

My last trip of the season finishes toward the end of August. It begins in cold rain, and we have to settle for a late, muddy camp on the first night, and even when the weather breaks and the sun comes out and warms us on day three, it is no longer the sun of summer. There is a golden aspect to the light it casts—not the white heat of July, but angling down as if we've already spun inexplicably toward autumn. When I wake that third morning to put on the coffee water at just before six, it's fully dark and the air tastes crisp. We wear hats before breakfast, and long fleece pants, and we hug ourselves against the chill.

The river is at its most beautiful this week. It's dropped more than seven feet since my first trip back in June. The spring runoff of silt has settled out and the water runs clear and cool on a hot day, but almost warm when the temperature outside grows chilly. The water is tinged green, and as we float we can look down through it and see the rounded stones on the river bottom, moss clinging to their sculpted curves. Boulders have emerged and gravel bars split the river in places and everywhere you can see the structure of it, what lies underneath the current, what inspires the water to act as it does.

Rapids take on a different character, too; they are tighter and more technical, restrictive and infinitely more beautiful as the rocks rise up from the channel and tongues of green water run between them and over them and the water folds back to create bubbling white holes. We have to work to get the boats downstream, bumping and wrangling through the rapids and reacting to every new rock, and also turning backwards and pulling hard at the oars in flat sections. Evenings fall earlier, and cooler, and often we barely finish the dishes before the first stars pop on above the ridges across the river from us. We build fires most nights because the air grows cold. I dream about apples ripening and the leaves turning gold and red back in New England where I went to school. At the same time that I long for my other life, the concept of home seems uncertain to me. I am no longer sure of where I belong.

Back in town after this final trip, in Lewiston, things feel different, too. Sitting around Boatland or having dinner at Thai Taste, the other guides talk about semesters, jobs they must return to, distant cities such as Flagstaff, Portland, Seattle, Moab. One by one the bicycles hanging above the commons, in The Room of Doom, disappear from the racks. The mailboxes, which have been stuffed with bottles of liquor and letters from home, gear and sun block and river toys, notes from other guides and trip photos, are mostly bare. Some folks have already torn off the tape that held their names and claimed the box as their place for the summer. The three bunk rooms are mostly empty of personal effects and the parking lot out back is half empty of cars and full of dories done for the summer: Tenaya. Chattahoochee. Lake Tahoe. Glen Canyon. The Morro Rock, my old, good friend.

I spend another week in Lewiston, waiting for my flight home to New York. I look for visible signs of change in myself: I feel and look stronger, for sure, although I've lost weight. My skin is dark and healthy and my hair has turned noticeably blonder. I am most proud of the Teva tan lines on my feet—white bars where the straps of my river sandals have kept my skin the color it was last winter in Manhattan, starkly pale against the deep brown color I've changed to around them. And at the base of the last three fingers of each hand, hard, pliant calluses have grown up, evidence of many long days of hard work on the oars.

I look for these outward signs of change because the inner ones are far more difficult to see—although I know they're there, too. I feel differently about myself and the world around me and know for certain that having spent these months here, nothing will ever be quite the same for me again.

Some of the changes, some of the realizations, are clear: that I could stand to improve as a boatman in many ways, including educating my passengers about the river with far greater patience and understanding for who they are and where they come from and what the experience is—and could be like—for them. That I need to soften and open myself to the people around me. That I need to be clearer and truer about what I want from my life, even if that means being alone. That I've already made my break from the East and my life lies before me in the West, outside, and that I will soon relocate for the second and final time to Oregon.

But I also know that in places, the river still runs deep, and though I've floated it in these places, it hasn't revealed itself in such obvious ways. I know that it might be months—years, even—before I understand what it has to teach me. I still need to give myself over to the flow and pattern and rhythm of it to learn its lessons and hear its messages. The river is inside me now, I know, and I need only wait and see where the current takes me, and what lies beneath it.

Packing my gear in Lewiston, putting away my wet suit and dry bags, my strap kit and my beat-up river hat, taking my journal out of the triple plastic bags I'd wrapped it in; thinking back on the feel of camp some mornings when I woke at five A.M. and had the beach and the river to myself; or about warm clear evenings, as our group gathered smiling around the fire; or how the spray of whitewater off a dory bow could fill me with nearly unbearable pleasure—all of these things are oddly nostalgic, and already I know I'll remember even such small details fondly wherever the current takes me next. And I know that in city or backcountry, East or West, frontier or settlement, I will think of the river, picture its gentle curves and the ridges receding from it in blue-green lines. There is a comfort in knowing that no matter what aspect my life takes on, this river will flow freely here, and that I might come to this place any time, in sadness or joy, in celebration or atonement, in prayer or to offer my thanks, alone or with someone I love. The waters will run smooth and fast, and though it will be a different river coming down out of the mountains it will also retain its constancy.

It's clear to me that I will return here, as well as to other wilderness frontiers within me—whether next year or some time later—because I know that what the river says is what I need to hear: to know myself, to feel wild again, to confront my own limits and move beyond them into the untamed country on the other side. I also know that Frederick Jackson Turner was right about one thing and wrong about another: that the frontier *is* essential to us as Americans, and as individuals; but that it has not and will never close.

My spirit awakened this summer as it hasn't since I was a boy. I am young again and the world stretches before me like a promising bend in the river. I've stepped outside of my life and been reborn; I've come to know myself and what I'm capable of and what I want and need. What is possible. And now I can move away from who I am toward who I was meant to be. It's been a great journey, a grand adventure, and the trip has just begun.

I will return here in spite of the river's name; but I will never return the same again, and that, after all, is most clearly what the river says.

Selected Reading List

Abbey, Edward. *Down The River*. New York: E.P. Dutton, 1982.

Abbey, Edward. *The Monkey Wrench Gang*. New York: Avon Bard Books, 1976.

Abbey, Edward. *Desert Solitaire: A Season in the Wilderness*. New York: Ballantine Books, 1985.

Bailey, Robert G. *River of No Return: Historical Stories of Idaho*. Lewiston, ID: Lewiston Printing Co., 1983.

Beal, Merrill D. *I Will Fight No More Forever: Chief Joseph and the Nez Perce War*. Seattle: University of Washington Press, 1985.

Bergon, Frank and Papanikolas, Zeese, editors. *Looking Far West: The Search for the American West in History, Myth, and Literature*. New York: Mentor Books, 1978.

Bishop, James Jr. *Epitaph for a Desert Anarchist: The Life and Legacy of Edward Abbey*. New York: Touchstone Books, 1995.

Brown, Bruce. *Mountain in the Clouds: A Search for the Wild Salmon*. Seattle: University of Washington Press, 1995.

Brown, Dee. *Bury My Heart at Wounded Knee: An Indian History of the American West*. New York: Henry Holt & Co., 1991.

Carrey, Johnny & Conley, Cort. *River of No Return*. Cambridge, ID: Backeddy Books, 1978.

Cox, Chana B. *A River Went Out of Eden*. Lagunitas, CA: Lexikos, 1992.

Duncan, Dayton. *Miles From Nowhere: In Search of the American Frontier*. New York: Penguin Books, 1993.

Eiseley, Loren. *The Immense Journey: An Imaginative Naturalist Explores the Mysteries of Man and Nature*. New York: Vintage Books, 1959.

Fromm, Pete. *Indian Creek Chronicles: A Winter Alone in the Wilderness*. New York: St. Martin's Press, 1993.

Ghiglieri, Michael P. *Canyon*. Tucson: The University of Arizona Press, 1992.

Grossman, James R., editor. *The Frontier In American Culture: Essays by Richard White and Patricia Limerick Nelson*. Berkeley: University of California Press, 1994.

Hillerman, Tony, editor. *The Best of the West: An Anthology of Classic Writing From the American West*. New York: HarperPerennial, 1991.

Huser, Verne, editor. *River Reflections*. Chester, CT: The Globe Pequot Press, 1985.

Kittredge, William. *Who Owns The West*. San Francisco: Mercury House, 1996.

Lavender, David. *River Runners of the Grand Canyon*. Grand Canyon, AZ: Grand Canyon Natural History Association, 1985.

Lopez, Barry Holstun. *River Notes: The Dance of Herons*. New York: Avon Bard Books, 1980.

Maclean, Norman. *A River Runs Through It*. Chicago: The University of Chicago Press, 1976.

Martin, Russell. *A Story That Stands Like a Dam: Glen Canyon and the Struggle for the Soul of the West*. New York: Henry Holt & Co., 1989.

Marston, Ed, editor. *Reopening the Western Frontier*. Washington: Island Press, 1989.

Nash, Gerald. *Creating the West: Historical Interpretations 1890-1990*. Albuquerque: University of New Mexico Press, 1991.

Nash, Roderick. *Wilderness and the American Mind*. New Haven: Yale University Press, 1977.

Peterson, Harold. *The Last of the Mountain Men: The True Story of an Idaho Solitary*. Cambridge, ID, 1969.

Reisner, Marc. *Cadillac Desert: The American West and Its Disappearing Water*. New York: Penguin Books, 1987.

Sadler, Christa, editor. *There's This River: Grand Canyon Boatman Stories*. Flagstaff: Red Lake Books, 1994.

Turner, Frederick Jackson. *The Frontier in American History*. Tucson: The University of Arizona Press, 1992.

Wilkinson, Charles F. *The Eagle Bird: Mapping a New West*. New York: Vintage Books, 1993.

Biographical Notes

Jeff Wallach is the author of *Beyond the Fairway: Zen Lessons, Insights, and Inner Attitudes of Golf*, published by Bantam Books in 1995. Wallach's sequel to *Beyond The Fairway*, entitled *Journeying Toward Par*, will be published by Harmony Books, a division of Random House, in 1998.

Wallach has also written more than 300 articles, essays, and reviews for, among many others, *Outside, Sierra, Men's Fitness, Health, Discover, Popular Science, Rodale's Scuba Diving, Money, Travel Holiday, Diversion, Golf, Golf Digest, Golf Illustrated, Links, Northwest Magazine, Pacific Northwest Magazine, Portland Magazine*, the *Oregonian*, the *Denver Post*, and *The American Book Review*.